Living Expressions:

As the Spirit Moves

Duane Johnson
&
Lila Bartel

Living Expressions: As the Spirit Moves
by Lila Bartel and Duane Johnson

Editing and book design by: Smoky Hill

Published by: Smoky Hill

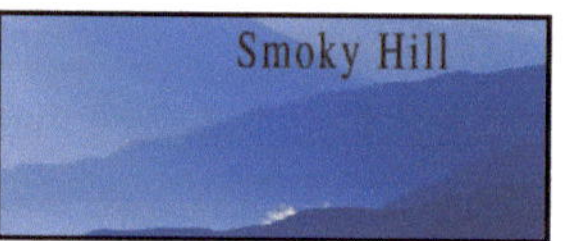

ISBN: 9 798985 224108

Stuck at home during the COVID-19 outbreak, watercolor artist Lila Bartel and poet Duane Johnson began sending their artistic expressions back and forth via e-mail. The two Kansans responded to each other's work as the spirit moved, and the result is this collaboration of illustrations and verse.

According to the Poetry Foundation, "an ekphrastic poem is
a vivid description of a scene or, more commonly, a work of
art." More generally, an ekphrastic poem is a poem inspired or
stimulated by a work of art.

Contents - Poems

Contents - Paintings

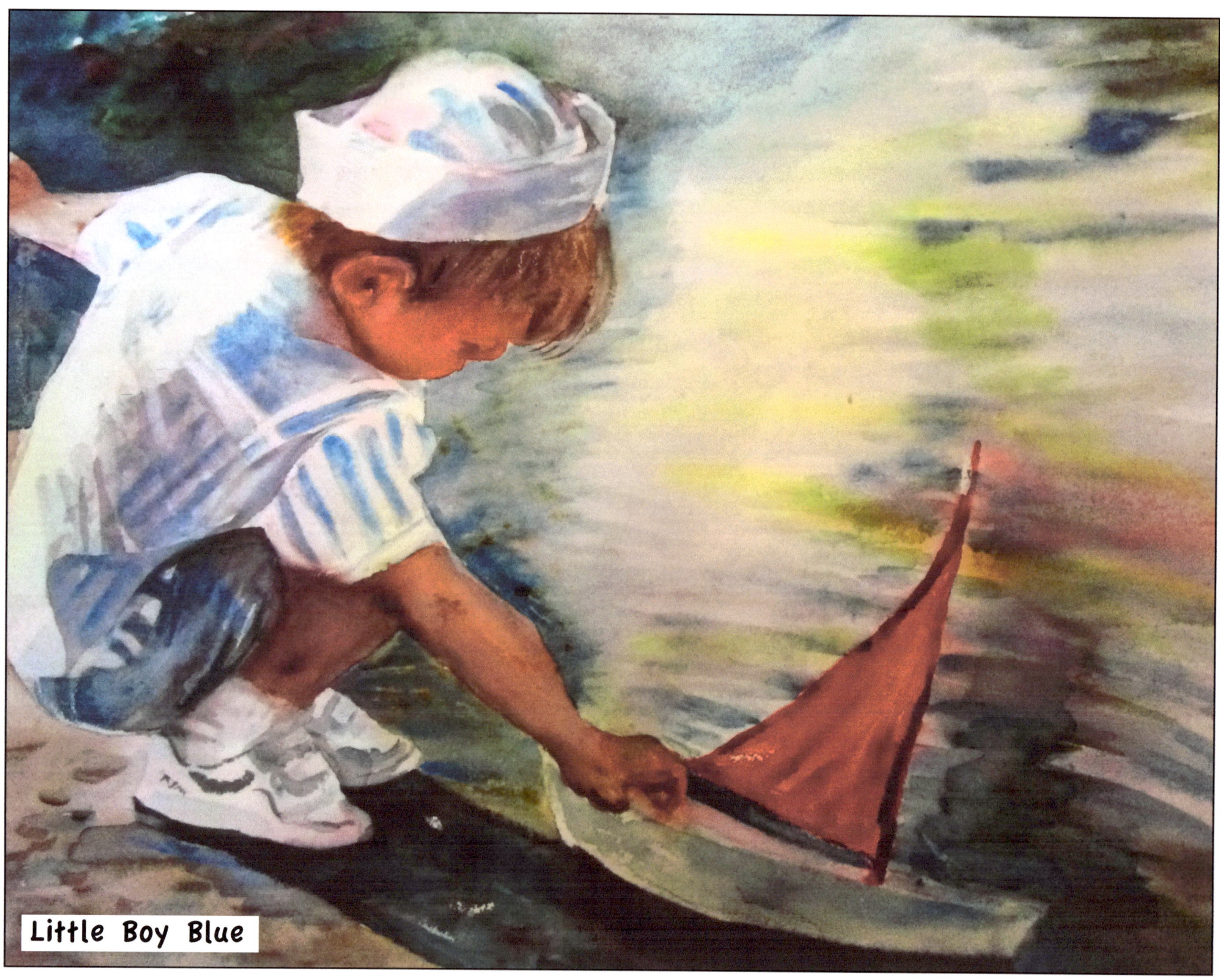

Little Boy Blue

Windsailor

I've known the man since he was young.
Back then, he reached away, full-sail,
from islands of solid thought.
Still, though it annoyed him to admit his fear,
he tried to hold fast to his Wind-driven
task of believing.

His ignorant allegiance graduated
through a few degrees
of pain. Still, faith stayed, and he began,
in autumn's sun-drenched blush, to hear
and learn to catch his spirit's zephyr, and hone
the craft of seeing

what good science can't ignore.
Now, he ploughs his seas of faith, close-hauled
toward his finest thoughts,
and more often is it becoming clear
that making fluid transitions is
the art of sailing.

In the Falling Snow

When does the circle begin?

I pondered this most recently on Sunday
when, while fishing for distraction
from a cancerous prognosis, it began to snow.
Flakes meandered down until they melted
in the river to begin another cycle.

Or, does the cycle end with river flowing
so that the circle recircles when
water turns to vapor?
Or, is the final segue vapor rising?

These thoughts were still revolving when
the start of darkness sent me home to sleep.
Then dawn on Monday woke me with
the answer, which I immediately forgot, so now,
once more, I'm in the dark about which phase
is the start. But regardless of what works
I do or fail to do six months to a year from today

this simple fact, at least, I know:
my faith is in the falling snow
whether it bring ending or beginning.

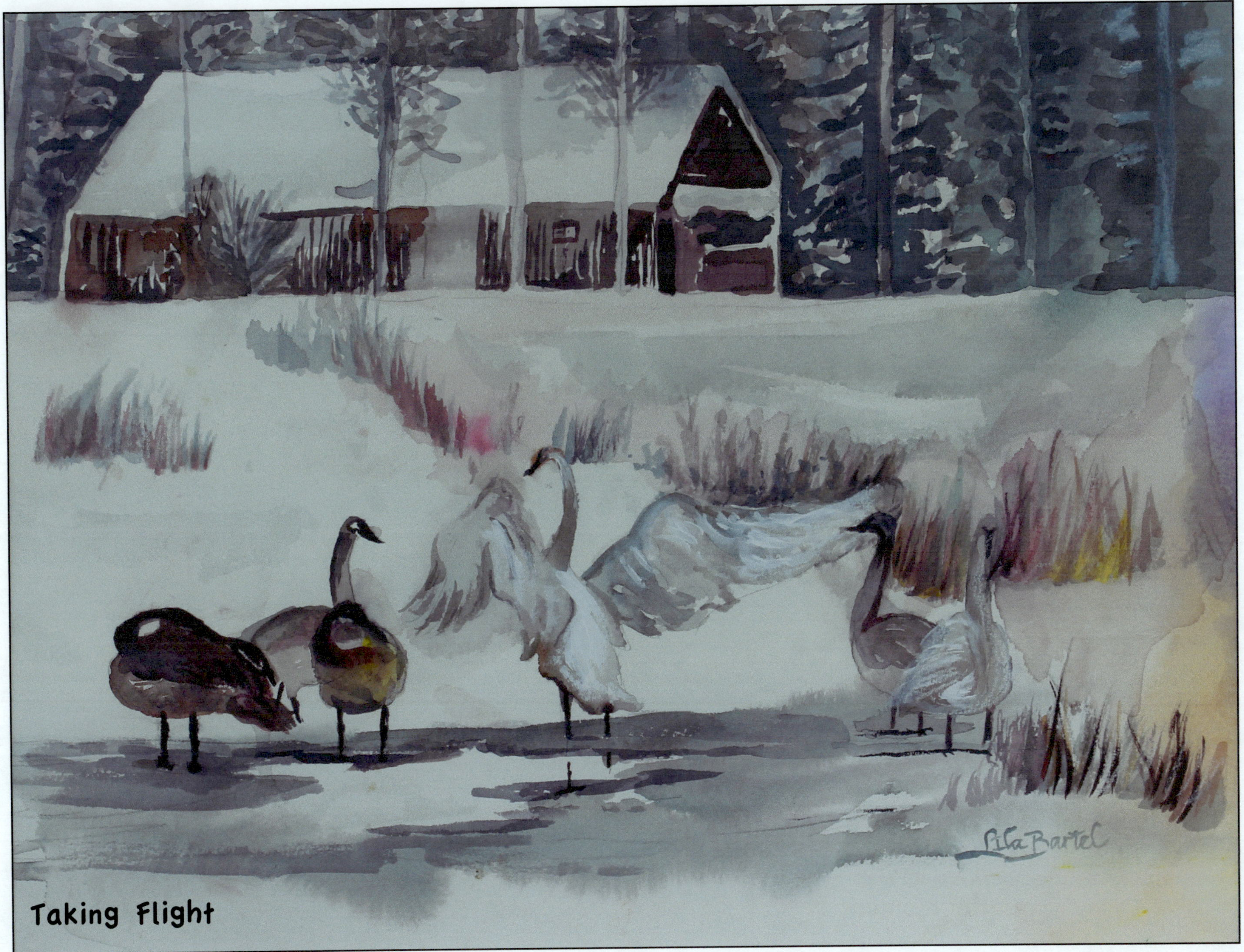

Taking Flight

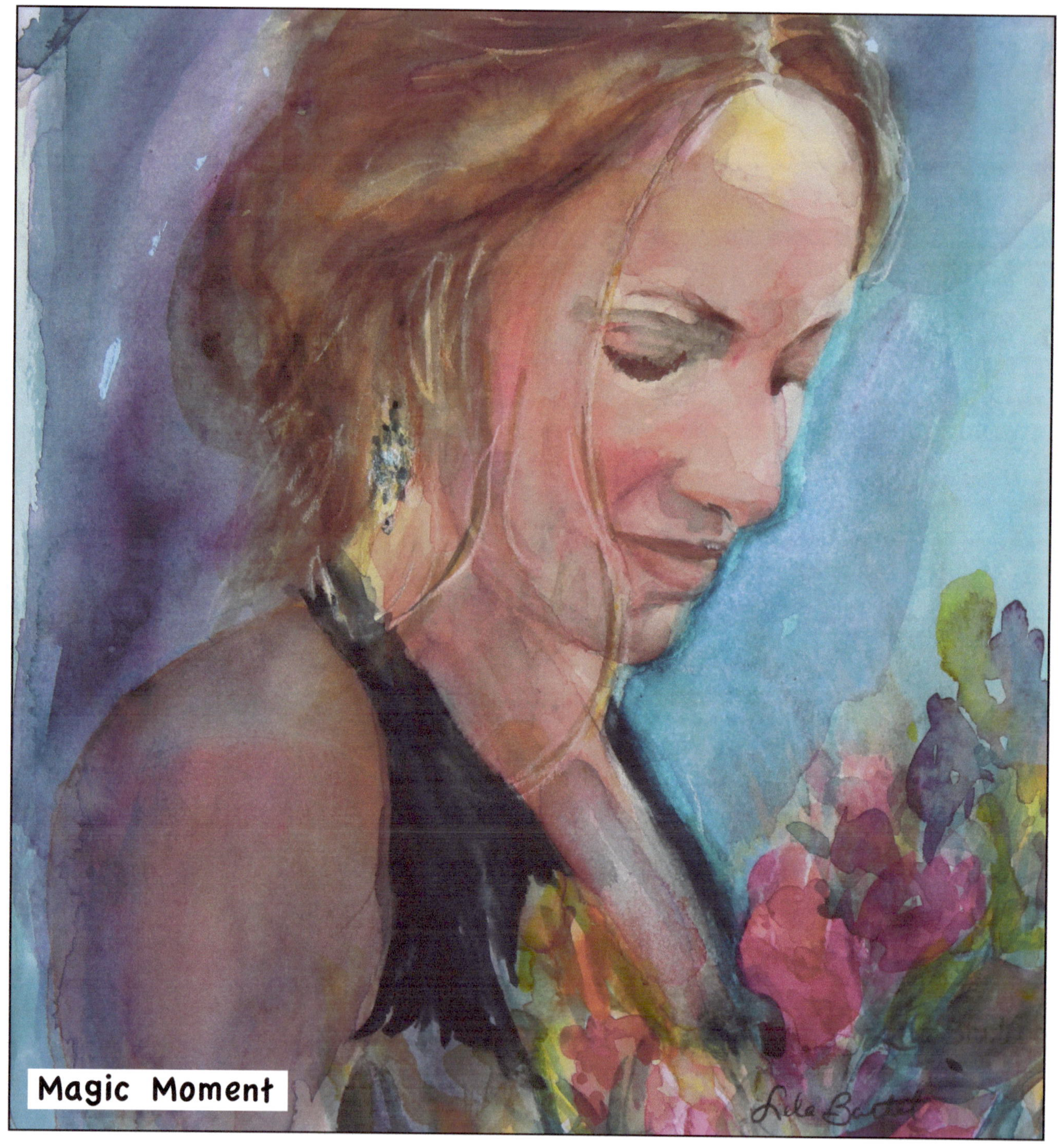

Magic Moment

I Did It!

When Pam asked me to take part in her wedding
I thought, "I'll never fit into this dress."
For the past two months I've cut calories
in half, resisted my favorite foods,
and exercized like a demon possessed.

It was tough, but I did it! Now, here I am,
having just caught the bride's bouquet
and as I admire these lovely flowers
and inhale their wonderful perfume
I have to admit, they look delicious.

This Seedling in My Hands

New life springs up as heaven's love flows down,
like Michelangelo's "God Touching Man."
My daughter's home will be a nursery of love,
a greenhouse for this seedling in my hands.

If each soul's fate lies in God's outstretched hands
we are His fingers pointing toward the source.
If each child is a stream that seeks the sea
we are the banks that guide the river's course.

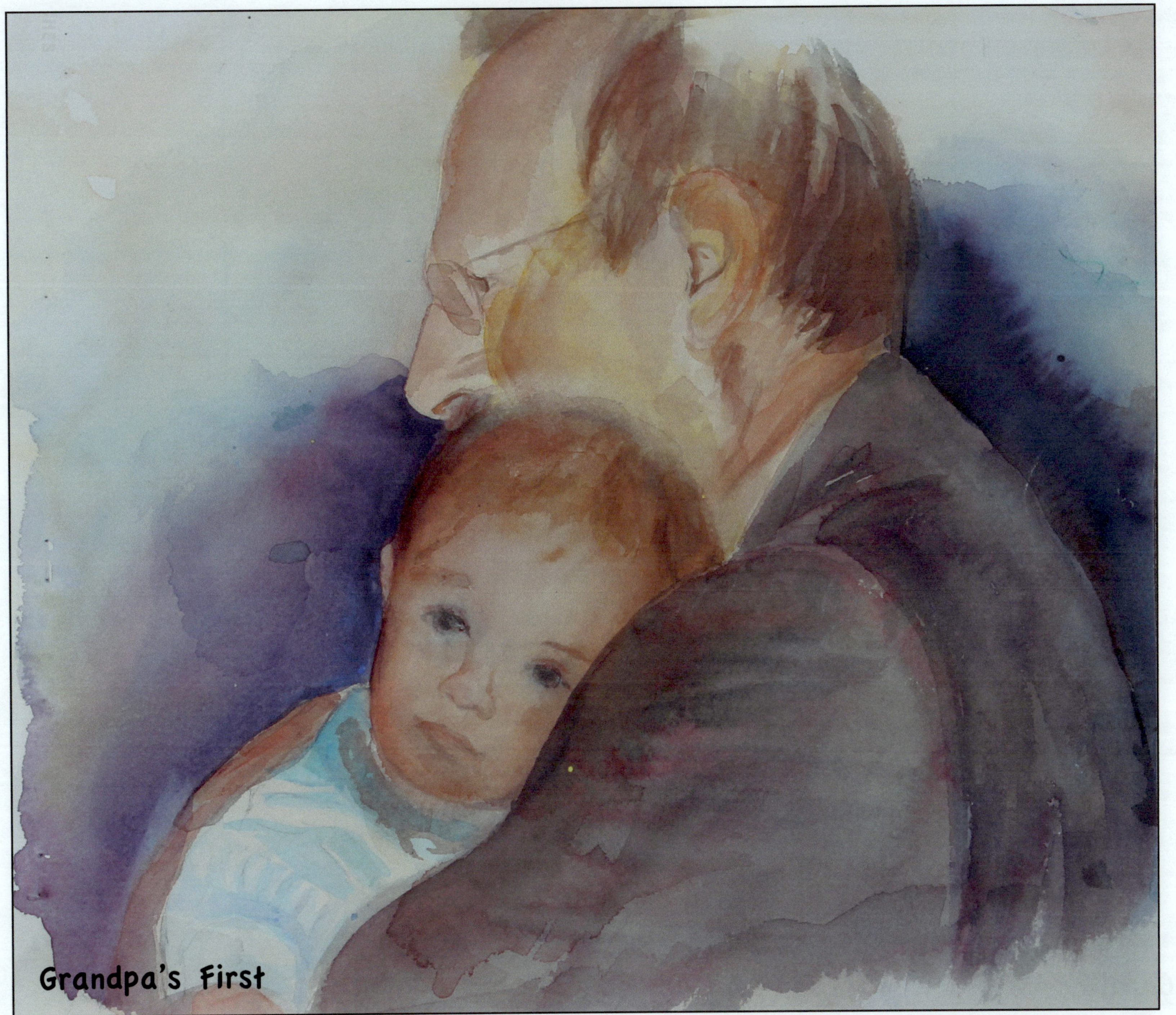

Grandpa's First

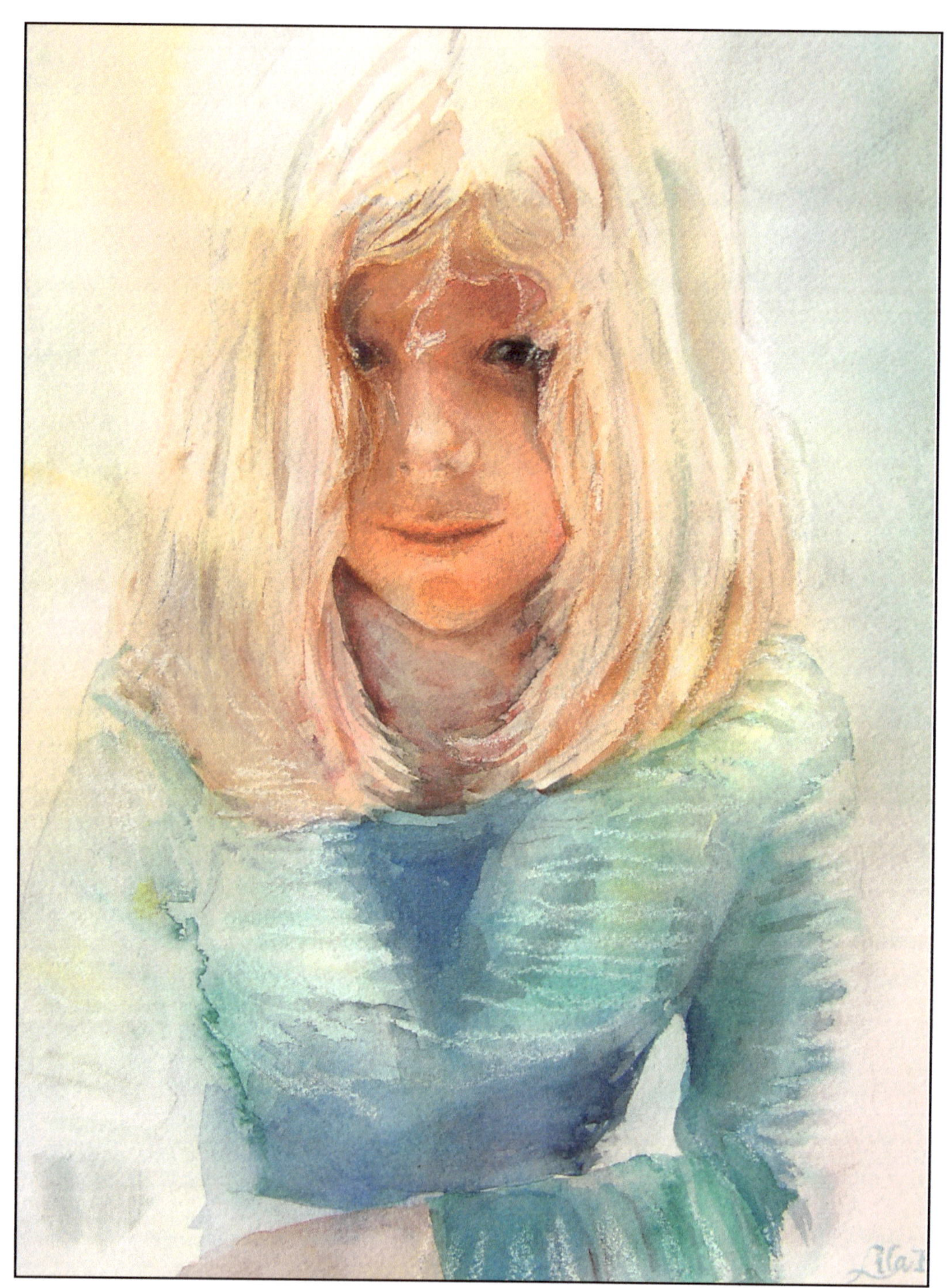

Caroline

Shimmering

She was like water on concrete

that sparkled in the sun

when the wind blew

a shimmering wisp of mist

in the rising light.

Big Responsibility

I can tell from the way Mom smiles
and speaks to you— warm like milk—
that you're going to need protection
in this neighborhood.

You've got a lot to learn
but I also have a lot of growing up to do.
What I learn today
tomorrow I will teach to you
and we'll grow together.

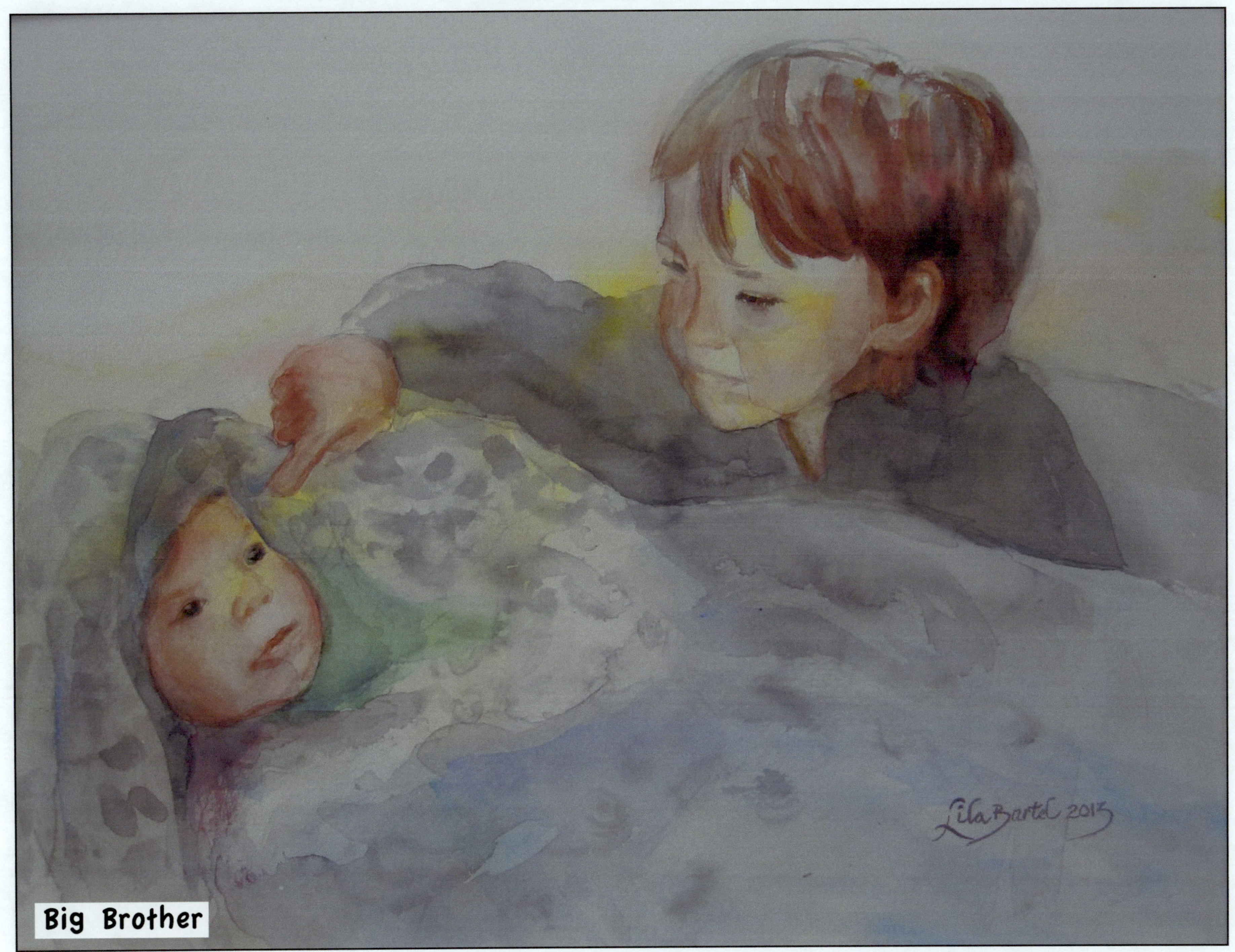

Big Brother

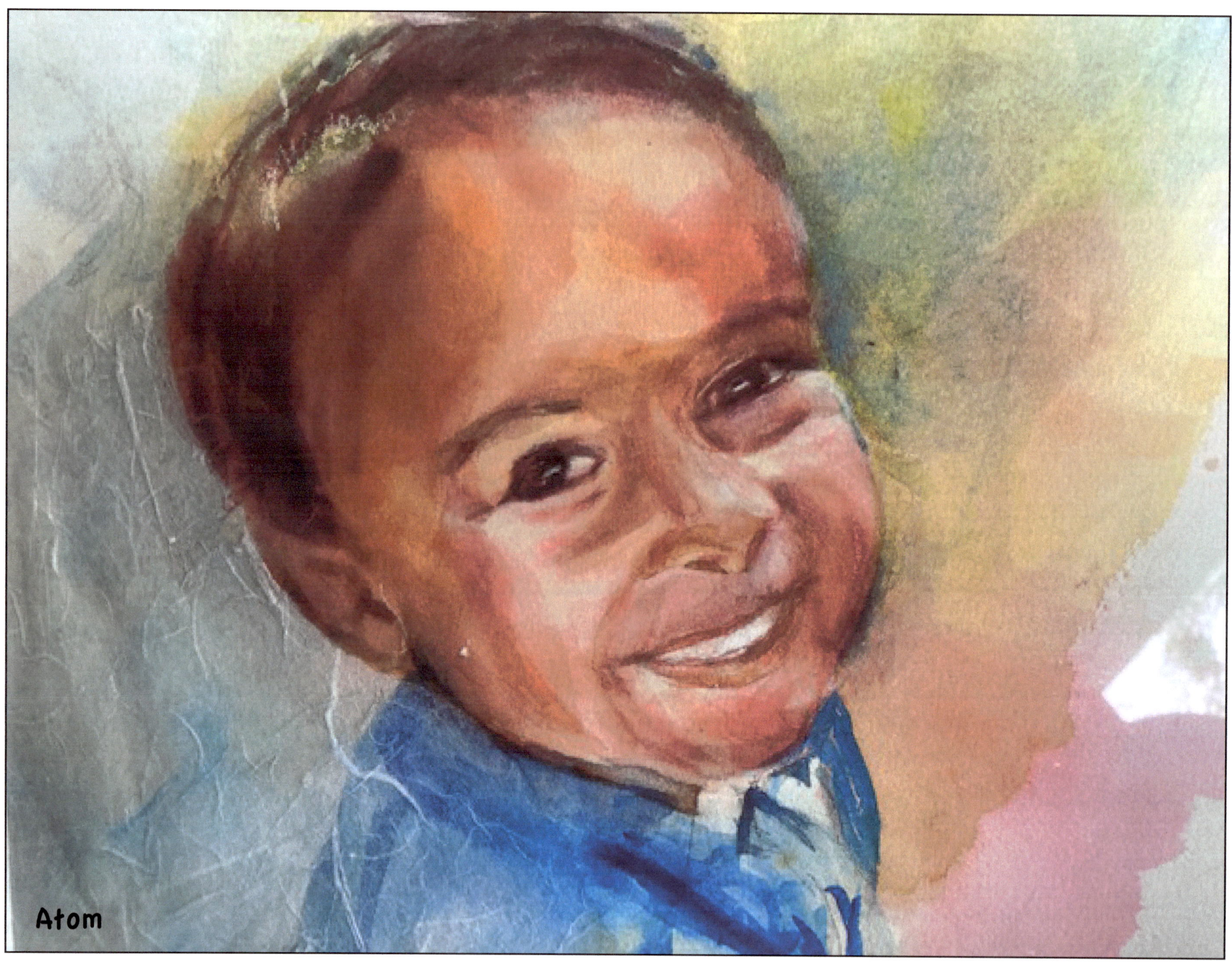

Atom

Anticipation

My dad
makes me feel glad

to be
young and free.

Today, he talked
about "The Talk"

he once had
with grand-dad

a Talk he'll one day have with me.

He said I would a- ap- appreciate
so I can hardly wait.

View from Smoky Hill

The view from Smoky Hill stretches unobstructed
by hickory, oak and maple.
In most directions, no Quixotic structures stitch the landscape.
Nor does smoke obscure this prairie partially checked by plows.

Well, perhaps on certain days,
as winged, serpentine mist ranges low above the languid river,
on pungent mornings when red-orange burns
Eastern horizons where they collide with lesser hills.
Then, predawn, "Sir Dragon" rises like the Flint Hills' patron saint,
intent on quenching foreign fires before they scorch the West.

I understand the river's fear of losing its possession.
Still, unhindered by current, I
can turn the other way and see as much, or more,
and, stretching even farther West
past unseen nascent mountains
I can sense an unplowed universe unveiling.

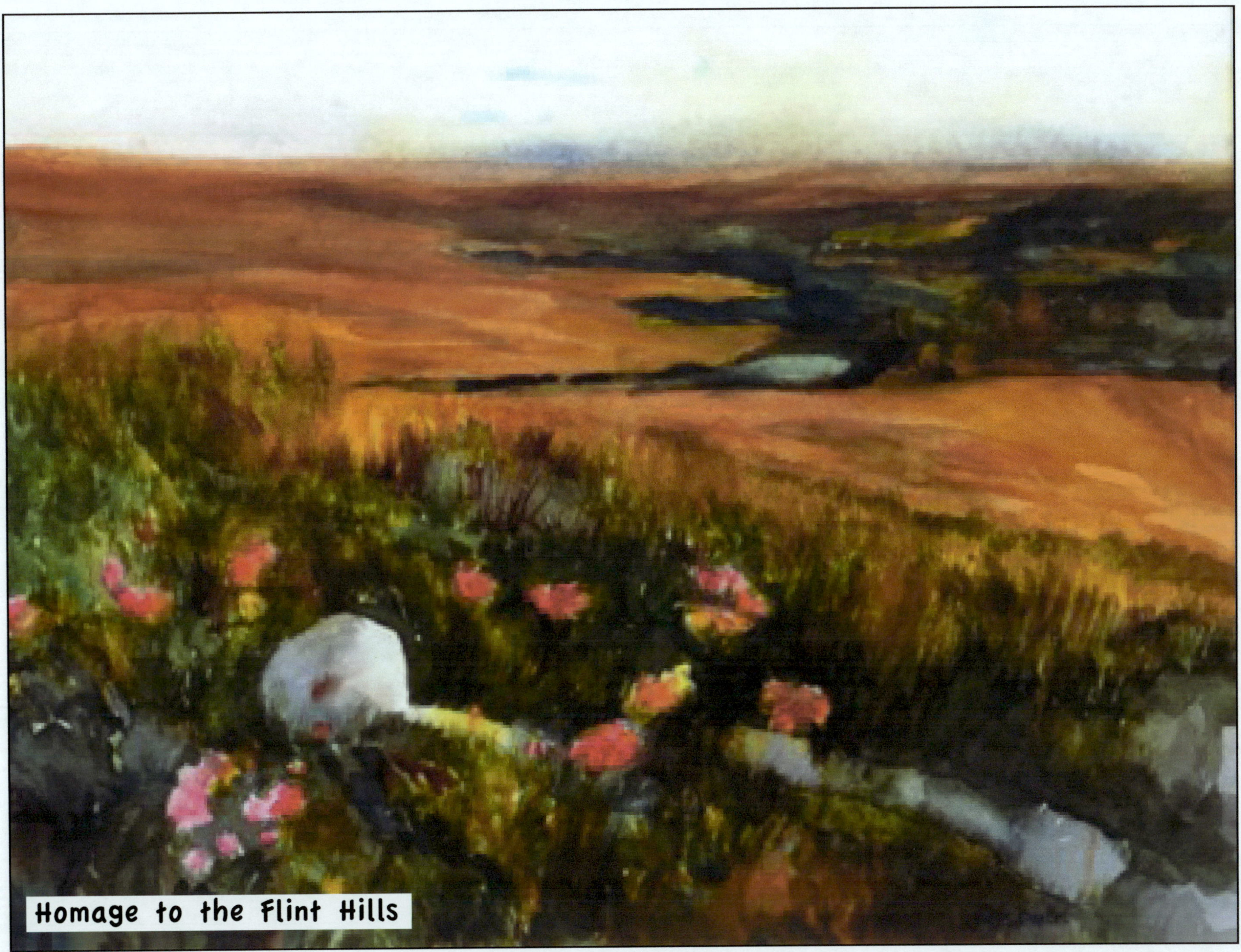

Homage to the Flint Hills

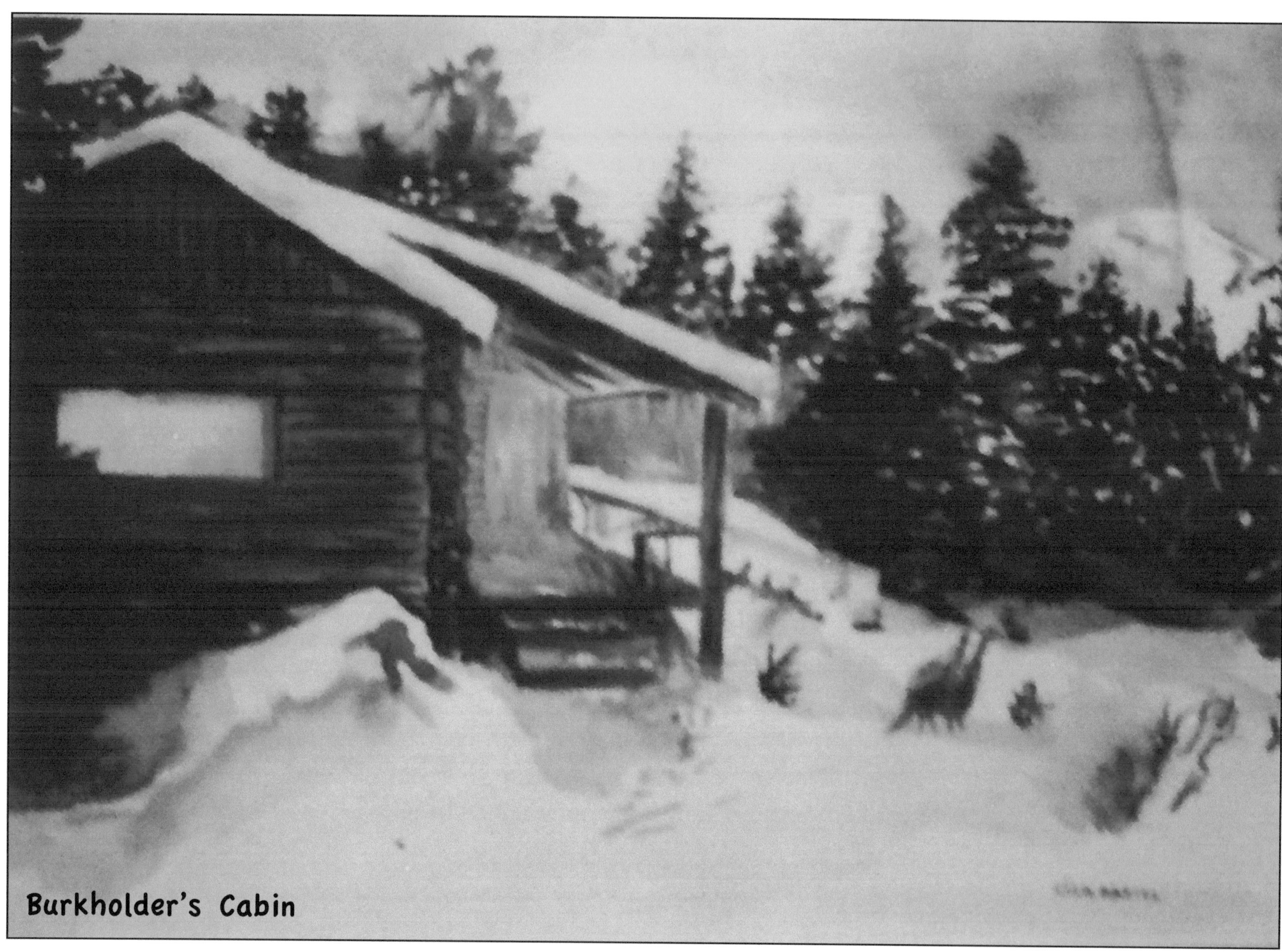

Burkholder's Cabin

Coming in from the Cold

It makes no difference if my cat's in the window.

When this valley's as white as the cat
the expanding outline of home
draws me up the powdered lane.

If I remember right
kindling tucked beneath the steps
dry wood fireside, and matches on the mantle.

I'll start a blaze
pour cider from a simmering pot, then
thinking of slippers Ellie knitted me for Christmas

I'll follow the cat as she slips from the window
patters into her favorite room and stops bedside
where, with closed-eyed satisfaction,

she'll purr and slyly watch me
admire her new-born kittens
sleeping warm inside my slippers.

Embrace a God of Goodness

Embrace a God of goodness
and you escape the desert
God who teases you
with life
then snatches it from you.
No Creator whose nature is to love
would bestow one single breath
without offering eternity.

So, embrace a God of goodness
and Easter morning dawns
self-evident
your eye of faith confirming
the tomb is empty.
Indeed, all tombs are emptied,
priceless contents claimed
not by worms
but by Spirit's flame.

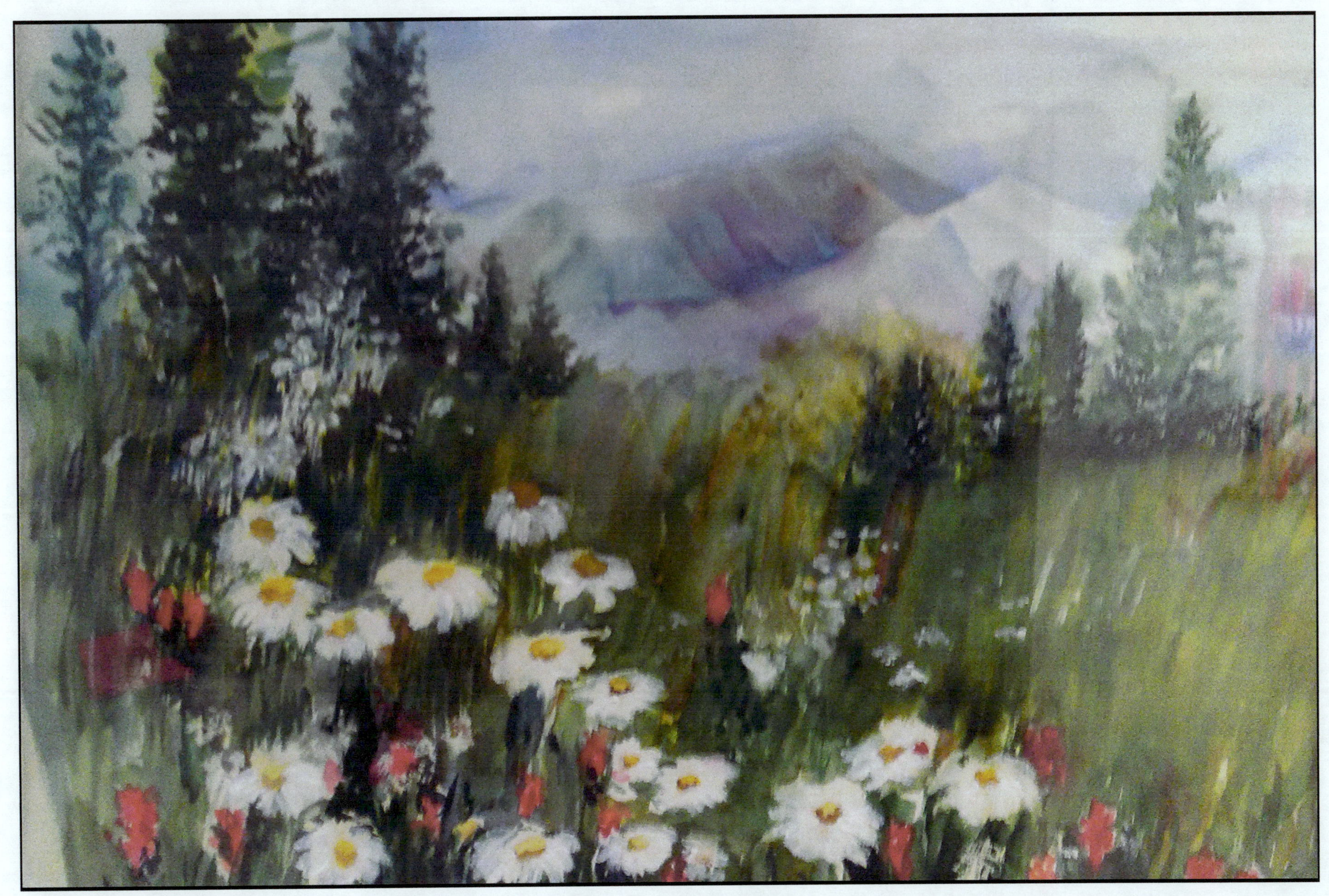

Elk Meadow

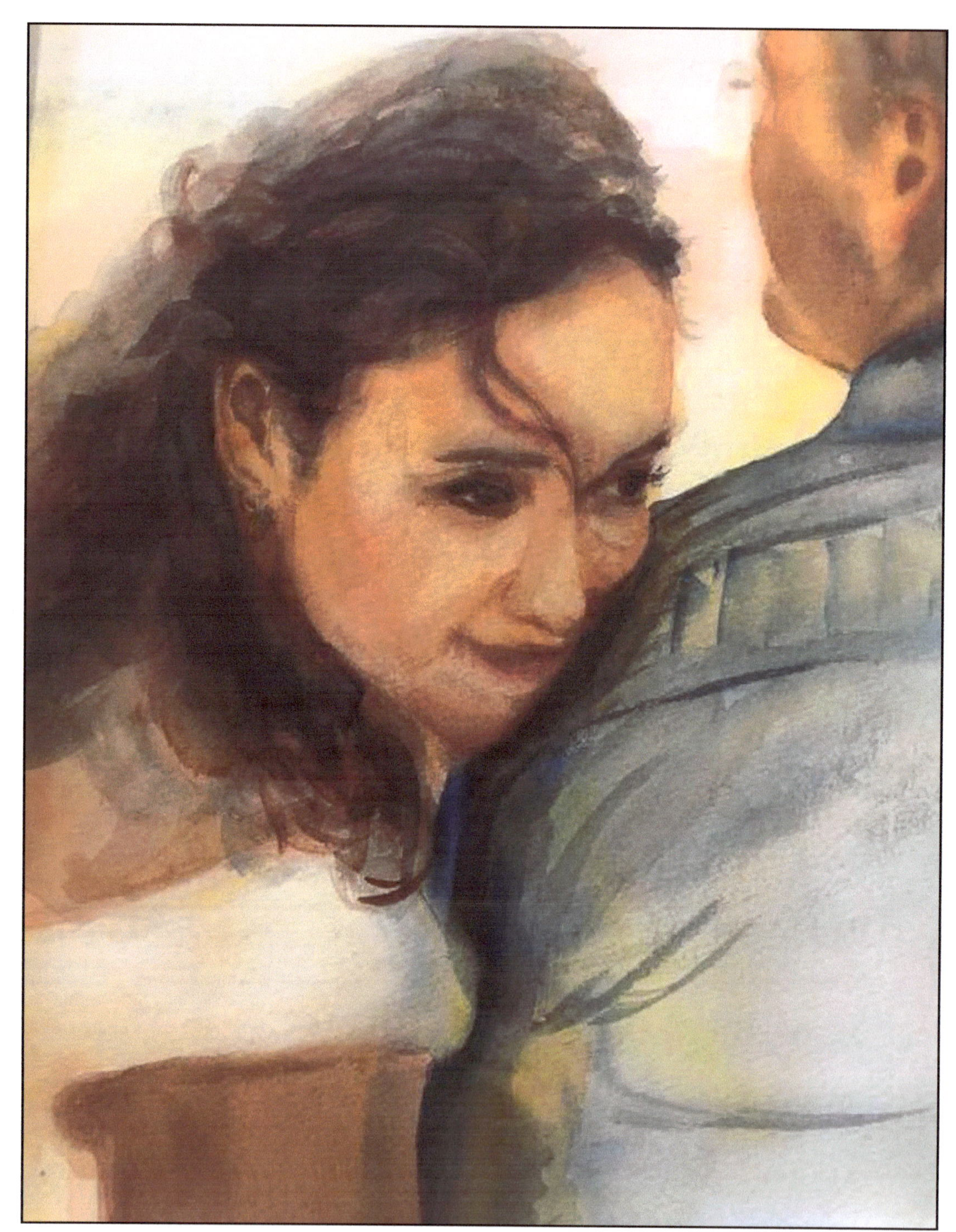

Let Me Count
the Ways

Invitation's Caress

In the grip of future finally known

this blissfulness,

please, never end.

Don't loosen your hold,

make your bosom

a cocoon for my soul,

let's be embraced forever,

always engaged

in invitation's caress.

The Flag

No accident of birth can sanction theft.
However low the fence or green the grass
the flag is not a permit to trespass.

When we pledge allegiance to one nation
we rend the seamless garment of justice.
Only unlimited love will suffice.

But all flags limit whom we care about.
They're barricades we've raised to shield our hearts,
dividing loyalty into subplots.

Someday, the Wall will be an artifact.
Someday, defences will come down for good.
That day, our hearts will pump a sacred blood.

Until, then we will have to contend with
dogs of fear, dogs that wag until they hate.
Those dogs will be redeemed, or hate their fate;

meanwhile, it's time to throw a flag on flags.
Tom Paine's "Rights of Man" provides us this clue:
there are limits to what limits can do.

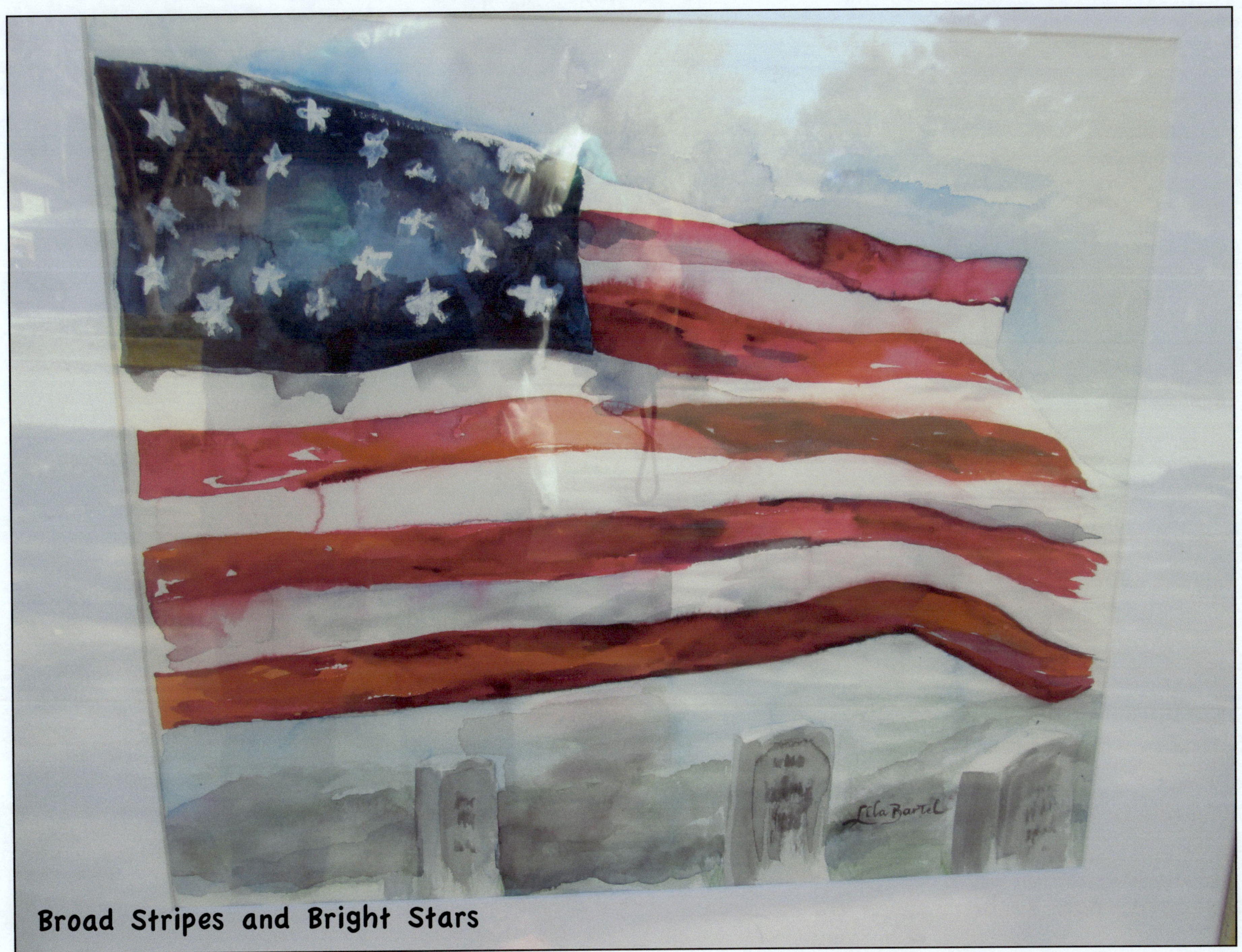

Broad Stripes and Bright Stars

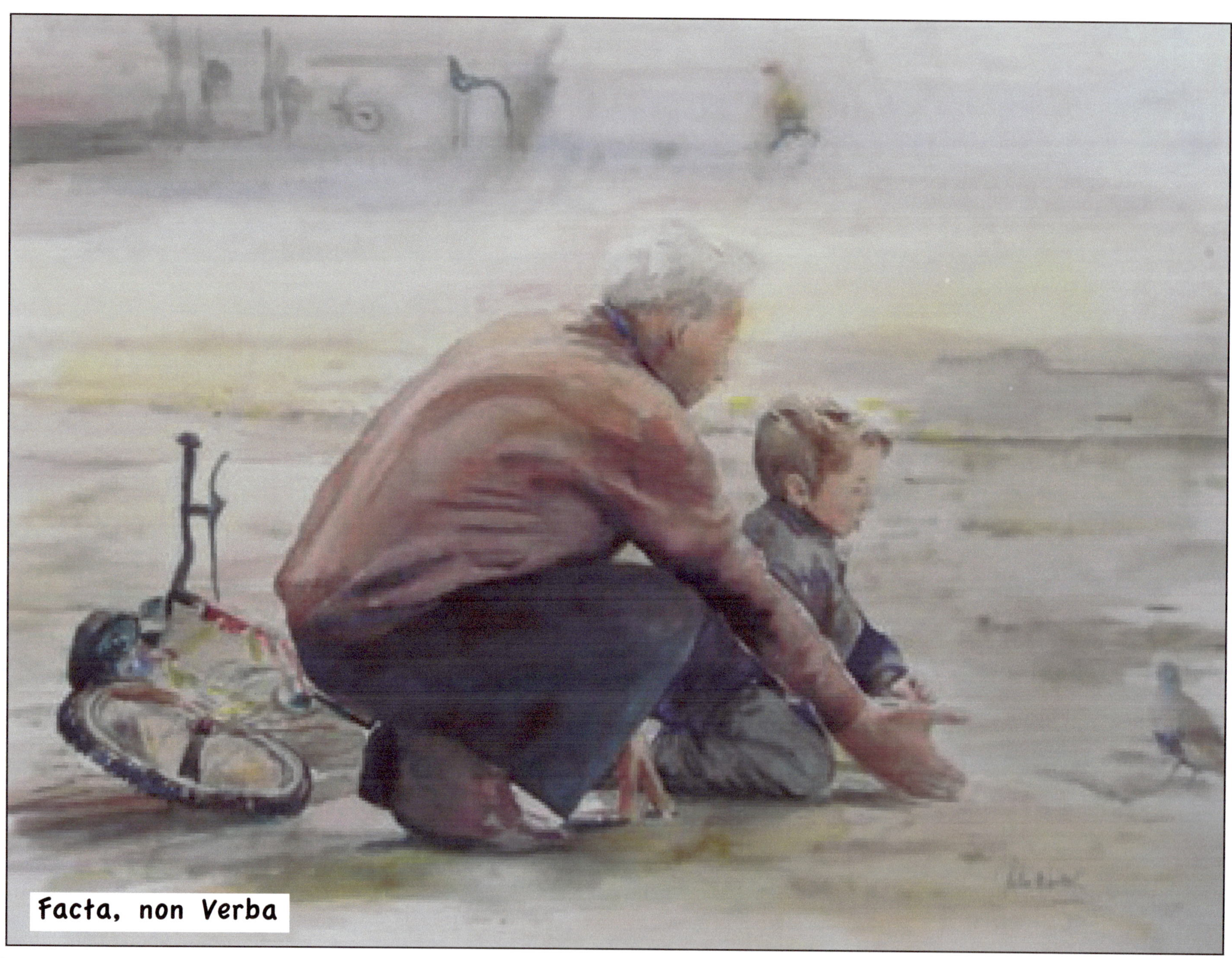

Facta, non Verba

Facta non Verba

"I don't know what it is, but Gramps is here,
so nothing bad will happen. His silence
in this huge, noisy world makes me feel safe.
Gramps only speaks when he has things to say,
unlike my sister, who babbles all day."

"He reminds me of his mom, unafraid
and quiet. We just interact with smiles
and hugs, just like his mom and I once did.
Some men make promises in pompous tones.
He'll be a man of action when he's grown."

Enraptured

The tossing and tumbling children do
    is the choicest role;
if they but knew, much harder they'd struggle
    to keep in view
what nature conceals on cue.

Heidi stared wide-eyed,
tracing every shape and sound, then capturing it.
She stuck to everything she felt, remembering.
Then, as if to show she understood, she giggled twice,
and tottering across the yard,
tugged me to attention as she slobbered,
"Yes see, Daddy! Name?!"

I then discovered in my core
a child entranced by nature's purls.
Open-mouthed and finger-curled, he coils,
enraptured by the world.

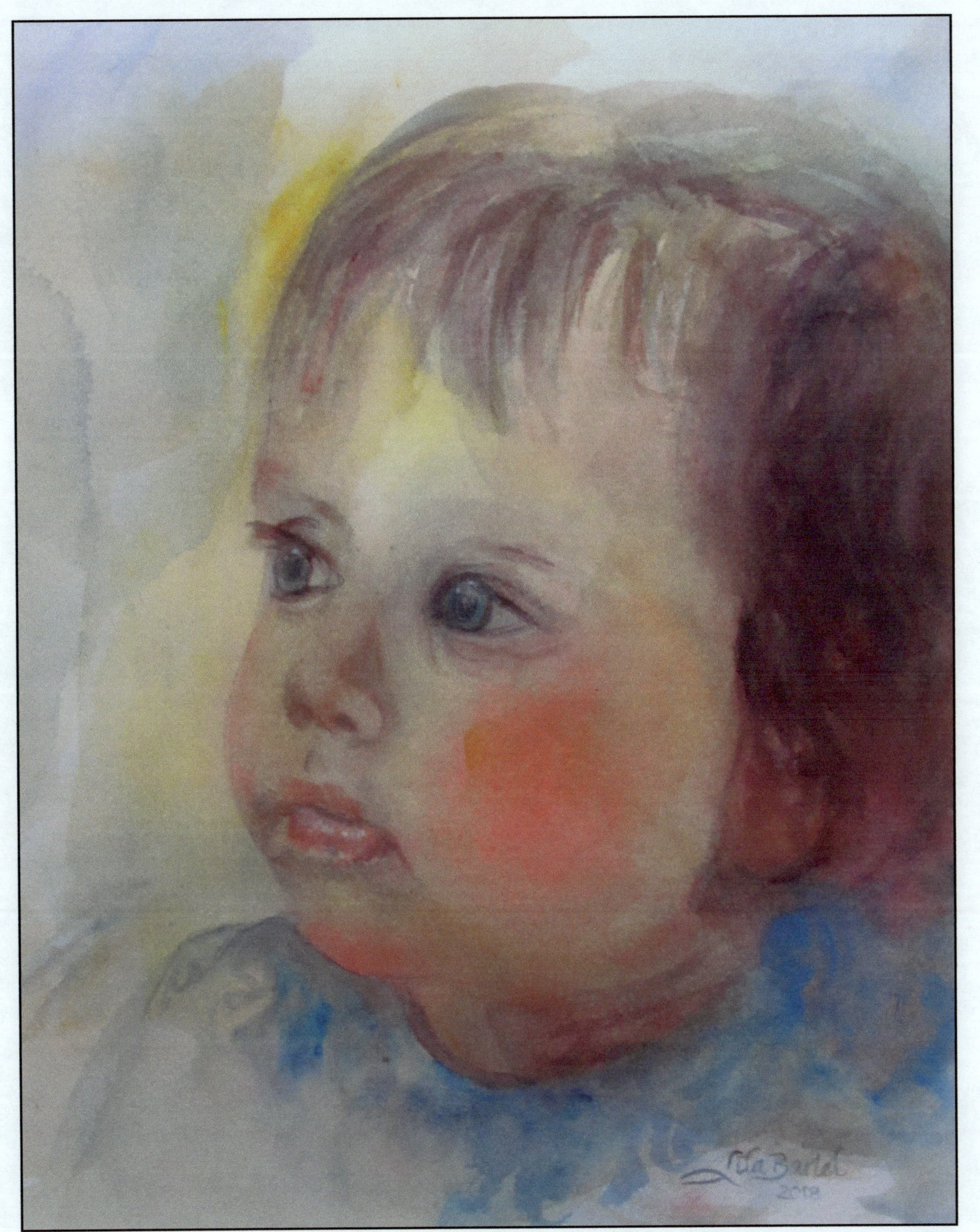

Enraptured

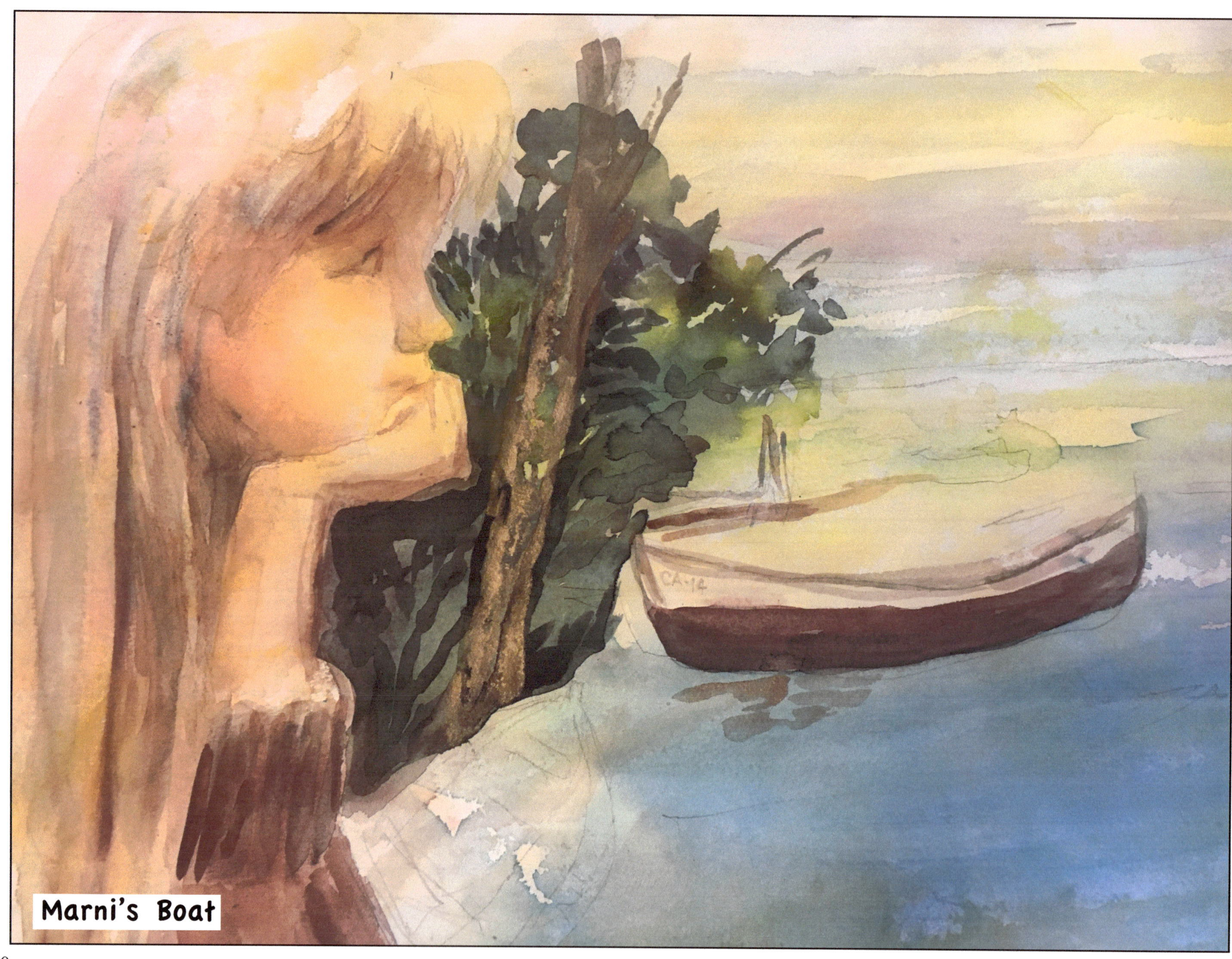

Marni's Boat

Marni's Boat

I'm told the boat, though old, has weathered well.
If I should die before its wake, ferried

to some free, uncharted destination
and sail into the Sound of silent love

to live the life my Father promised me
long beyond my age etched now on the bow,

Whom might I find? What would I leave behind?
And what might I accomplish in my Time?

His Timbered Choir

Today his timbered choir sings, bird songs
weaving their tunes with silence, in rhythm
with trees. It's Sabbath of course; no church bells
invade his river-edged wood. In red soil
of his Bluegrass farm, his tiller is still
today. Barn doors are closed, and he's strolling
in quiet relief from six days of toil.

This holy day will bow to Labor Day,
an extra respite paid to those who sweat.
I wonder what he'll do to honor time;
meanwhile, he has pad and pen to serve him
until the sun goes down. What to record?
What metaphors and rhymes might incubate?
What lyric will his timbered choir sing?

Immersed in sacred service through his verse,
he tunes his voice above the timbre's boughs
in harmony with spirits of the soil
then channels earth and heaven with his themes.
Disciples in his woodland chuppah's shade
vow to wed their future to creation
while living light streams through the canopy.

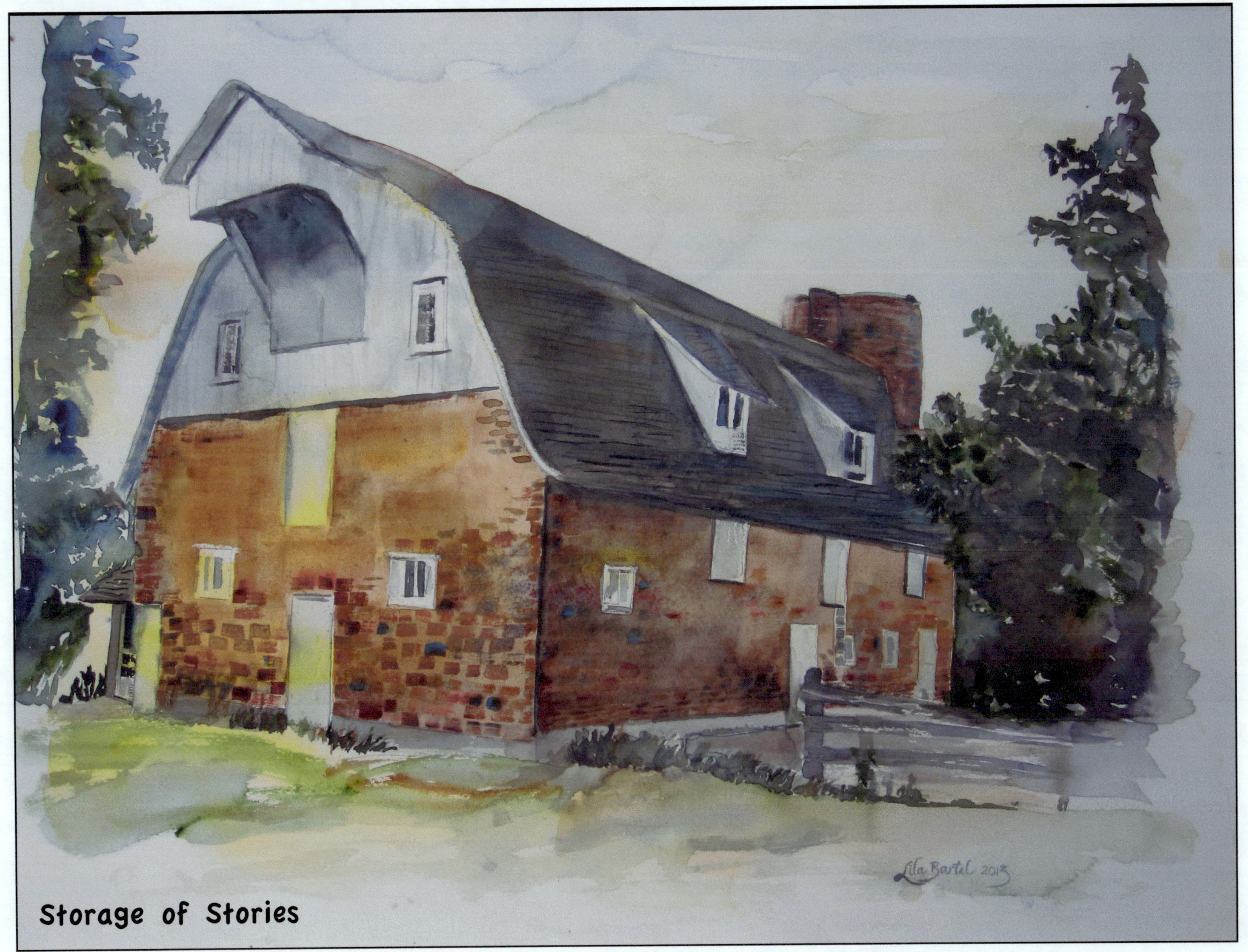

Storage of Stories

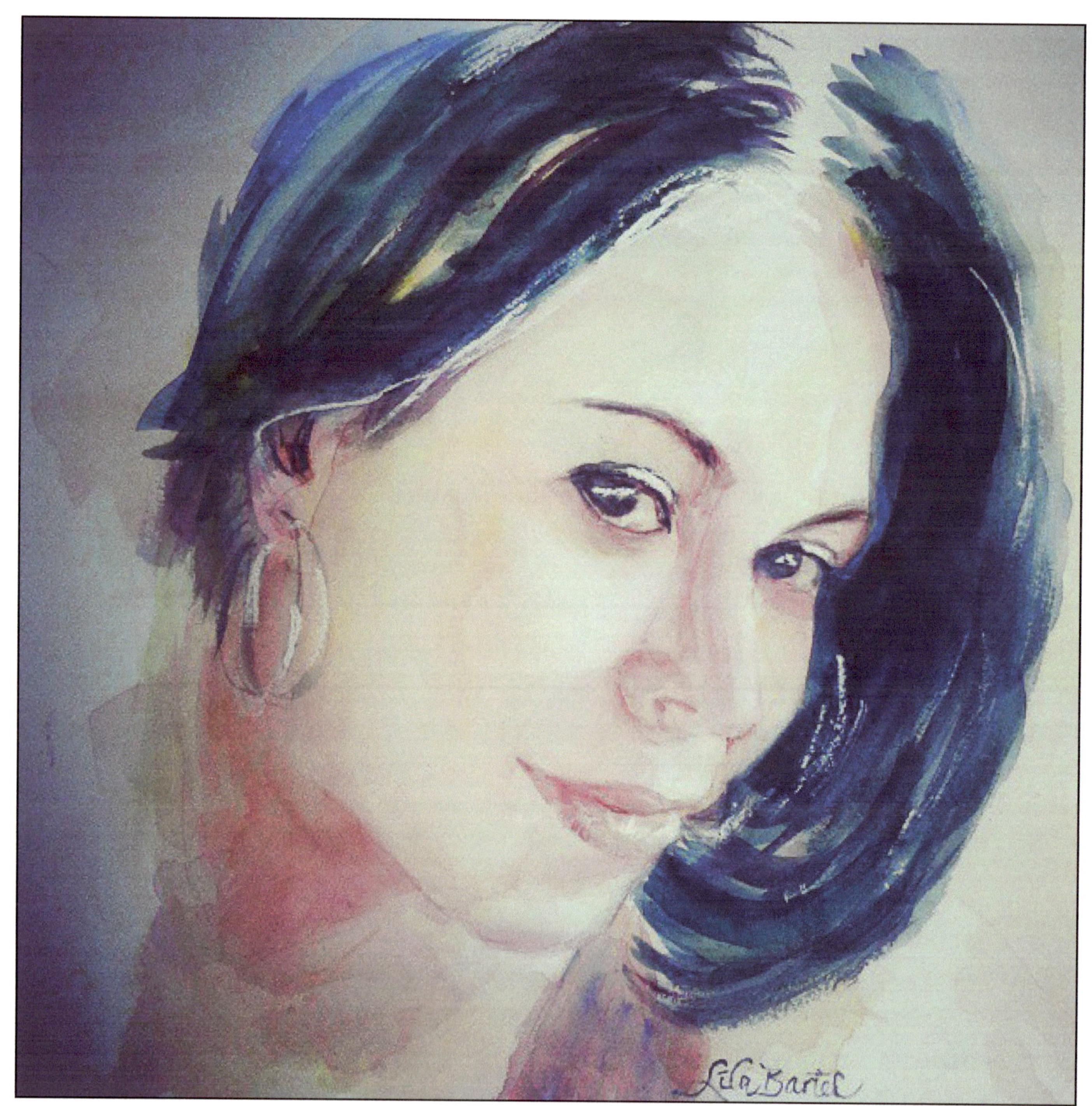

Olivia

Poet of Cocoons

Poetry, sometimes cocoon,

more often is ointment on a wound

called the human condition.

A fan of cocoons to ease transitions,

my suspicion is too much focus on the wound

leads to spiritual malnutrition.

So when I write, I spin cocoons

with a butterfly's ambition.

Some need salve to soothe the wound, I don't deny,

but if your embryonic spirit wants a loom

to weave a womb where it can lie

until you're ready for the sky

here am I, poet of cocoons

and midwife to your butterfly.

Cowling's Legacy

Jim and Ann now own this land,
at least that's what the title says.
You'll find my blood soaked in the soil
along with grandpa's, dad's and Ann's.

Grandpa built the house and sheds
the year before my dad was born.
The turkey barn was Ann's idea.
She named her first gobbler Red Fred.

So many stories I could tell.
The time Red Fred half killed the dog
The hayrack landing on the barn
and grandpa Louis in the well.

Bluestem grass was all he could see
when Louis staked his homestead claim.
He knew his hard red grain would thrive,
as has his Cowling legacy.

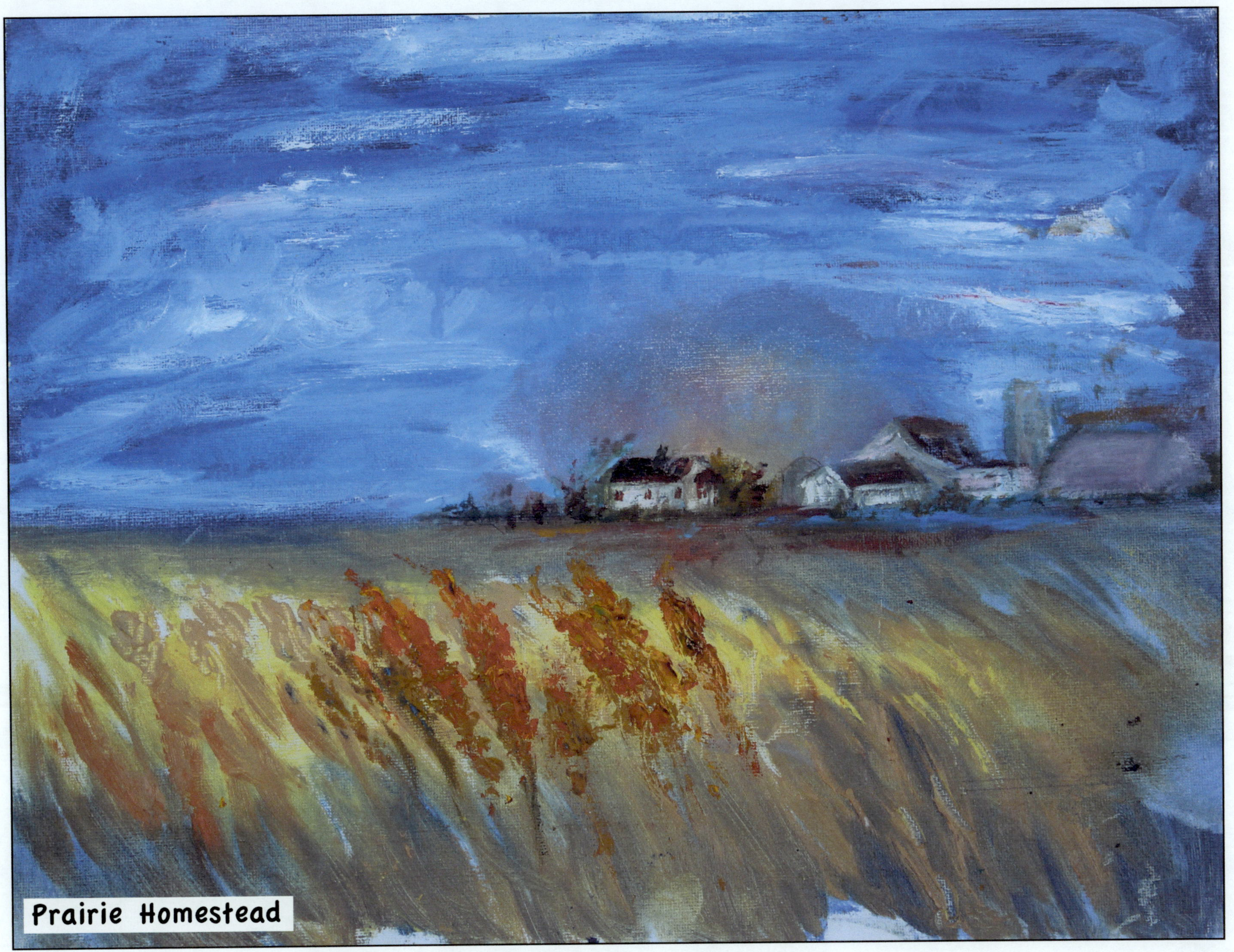

Prairie Homestead

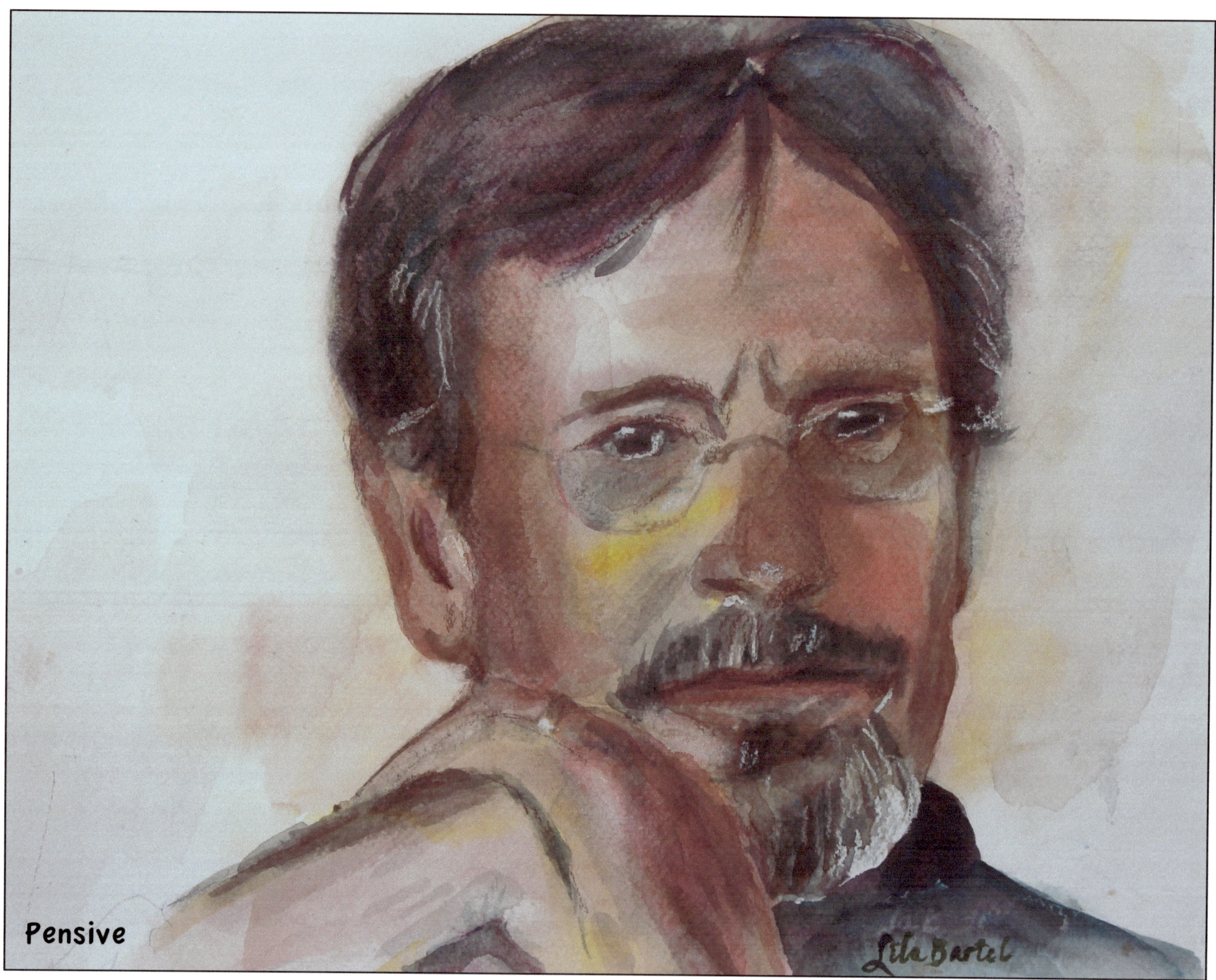

Pensive

Getting Struck by That Thought

Did you just get struck by that thought?
Did I glimpse it propel from this maple above us
and smack you as you glanced askance?

A thought is what I think it was,
"large and melodious," as our favorite poet said,
not that I've ever thought thoughts
quite like that.

But the poet was well acquainted with such thoughts.
By the time he posed his question, "Why?"
he'd moved on to seeking origins,
tracing his conclusions' breadcrumbs
backward to his soul.

As well as any, you understand
that poetry is your body and soul conversing
the way you'd like others to speak with you,
honestly, generously, joyfully,
like your sister to her lover.

Good Enough for God

Gravity aside, if a universe-size diamond
were set inches from my nose,
its enormity and nearness would confound me.

From such a disadvantaged vantage point
I'd scarcely know its value
nor appreciate its beauty,

but I would spy the flawed reflection in that perfect gem
then pray my sense of awe
is good enough for God.

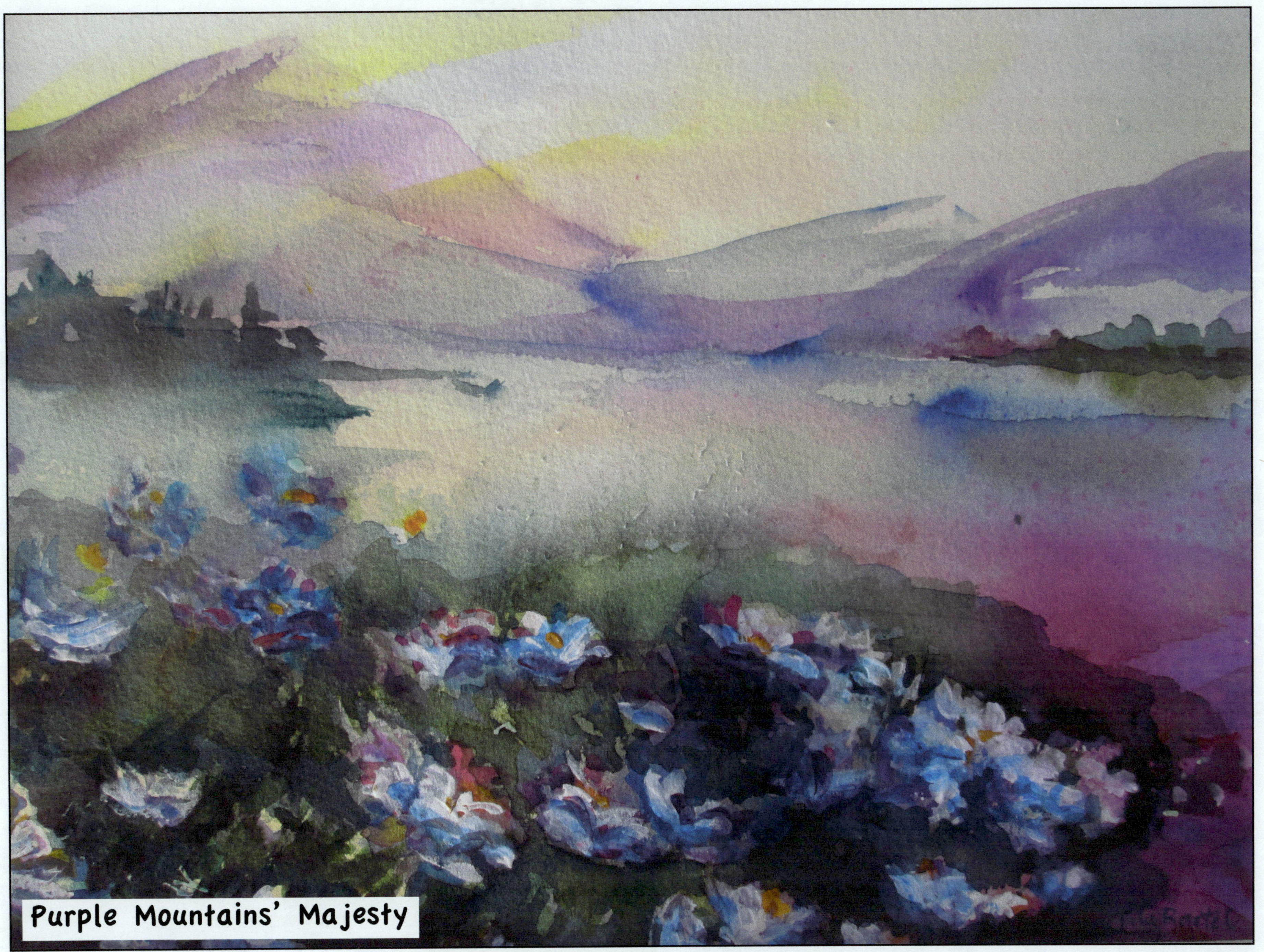

Purple Mountains' Majesty

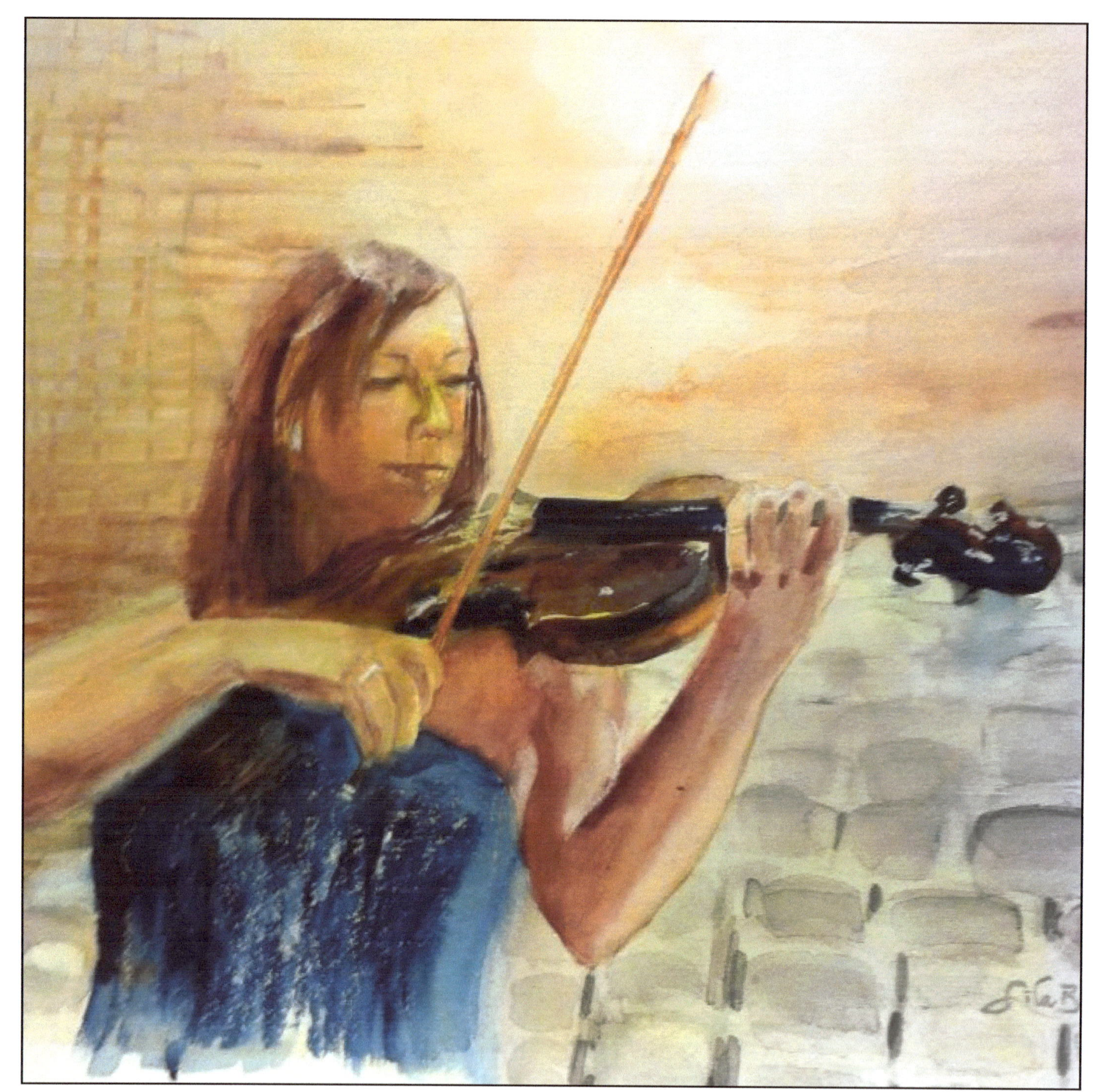

In the
Zone

Fresh on Fiddle

I heard an old story played fresh on fiddle
to a tune that might have been too hard to sing
    if it were true.

Then again, great composers know
there's truth and there's fact, siblings perhaps,
    but not twins.

In any event, that story has been countless times retold
without the fiddle, and so, the singer claims,
    has suffered greatly.

True enough, the fiddle seemed not to fully recognize
its old friend, thanks to changes in the tune time
    had cultivated.

But the fiddle, having been there, knows the original
better than the singer, and so is in the best position to
    choose between the two.

An Emerald Gift

I remember the mid-summer morning a hummingbird
flew whirring past me, as I stood
half-asleep and shivering in crisp mountain air,
reel in hand and hook in stream,
gambling my bacon breakfast with trout.

Entranced by twilight's colored quiet
and honey-suckled fragrance
I was following misty fingers drifting upward
escaping current
when suddenly, the hummingbird.

On singing wings, she emerged
from gray cliffs behind me,
and spotting me watching her, delayed
her greater purposes to play for me,
performing her aerobatics as if noting
some musical backdrop for her own ballet.

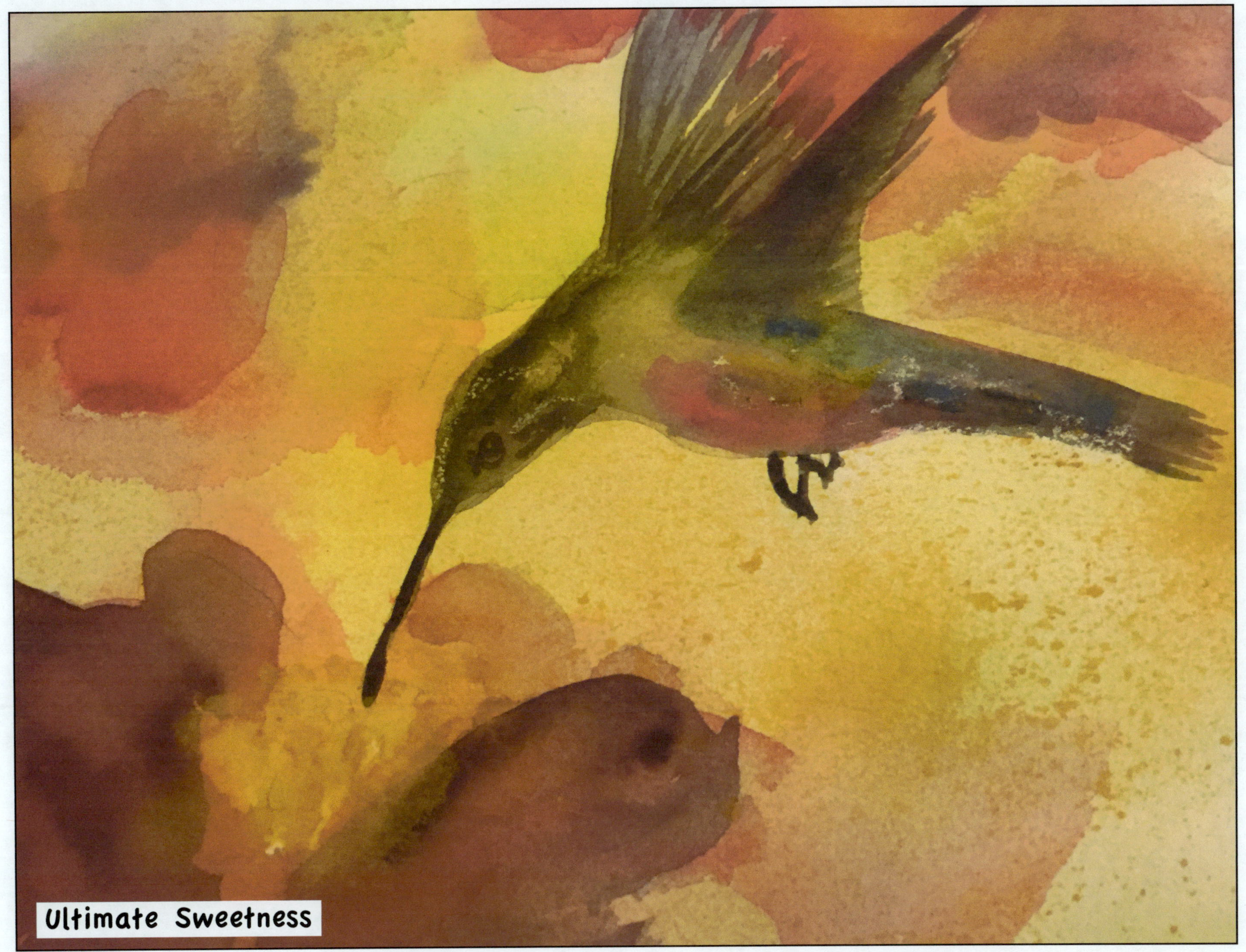

Ultimate Sweetness

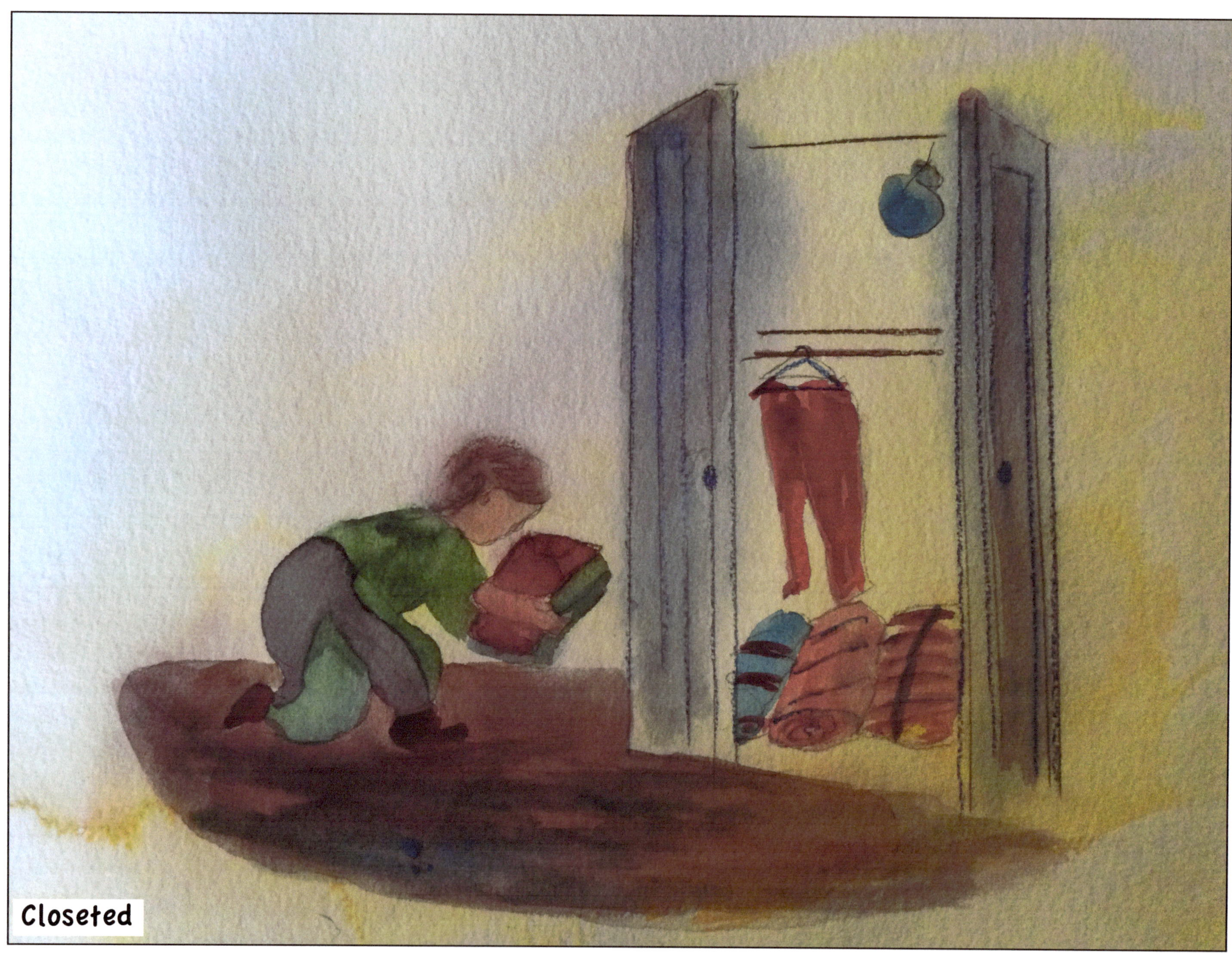

Closeted

Red Pants

They gave me red pants, then called me grandpa
when I refused, at age five, to wear them.

They could not understand my lack of taste.
I could not understand their hurt feelings.

So they thought I was rude and ignorant
and I thought they were rude and ignorant,

and they hung in my closet, those red pants.

Mountain Climber

He climbed too close to sacred peaks.

On Sundays we would shake our heads
and let him know how mad it was
to scale edges. Once we heard
him joke about a scarcity
of air at rarer altitudes.
And several times we watched him pray
while dangling from a precipice.

So, no one feigned surprise that day
Emanuel collapsed near one
such sacred peak. But dying slowly
gave him time to find his voice
and reminisce about grand vistas
none of us had ever seen
while trailing lower altitudes.

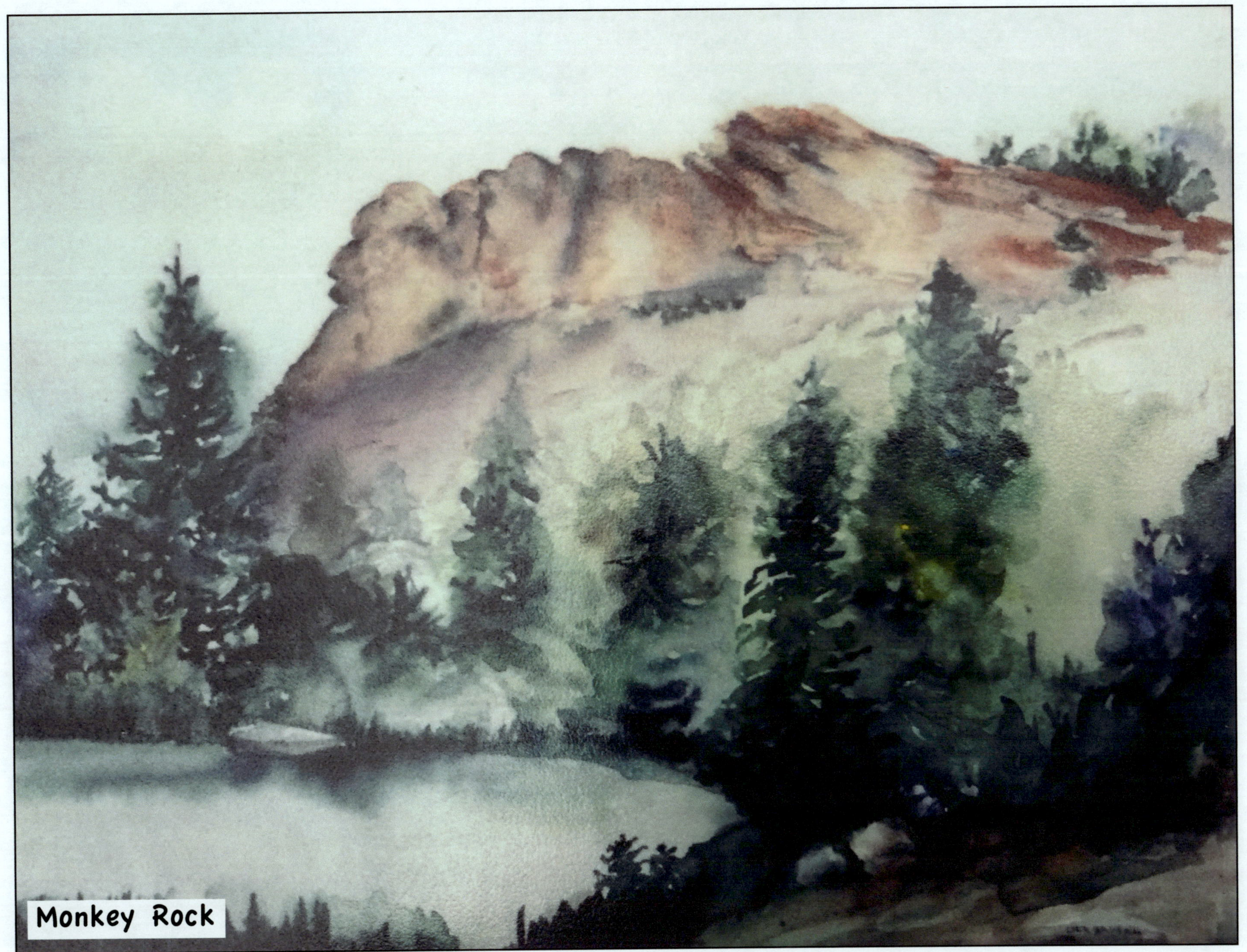

Monkey Rock

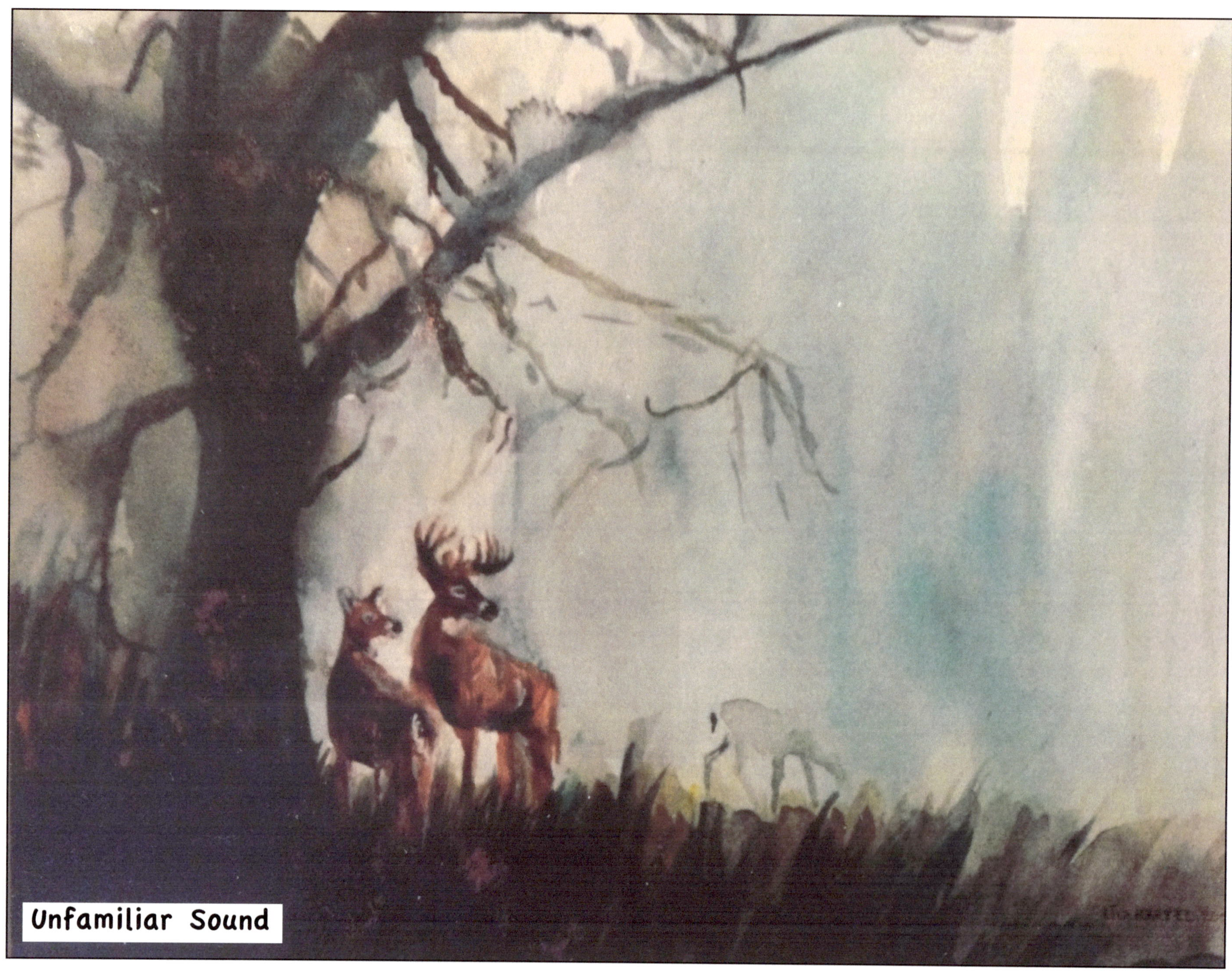

Unfamiliar Sound

Casual Reply

Once he heard a whispered sound
a sigh that flew too fast for words
a subtle breath-stroke so profound
it almost went unheard.

Boldly he obeyed its urge
to let past and future merge.
The speed of light could not contain
his mind within his brain

nor time and space hope to control
unmeasured motions of his soul,
which leaped beyond the pin-wheel plane,
a diamond spun from coal.

What You See Is What You Get

I'm betting you will blink before I do.
Don't play me like a grand piano, boy.
Perhaps you thought you'd sweep me off my feet?
You know where to stick it. I'm not your toy.

Don't bother with the "lines" you've memorized,
I've heard them all. The cleverest fall flat
when awkwardly rehearsed by clucks like you.
But I've a choice. I'd rather have a cat.

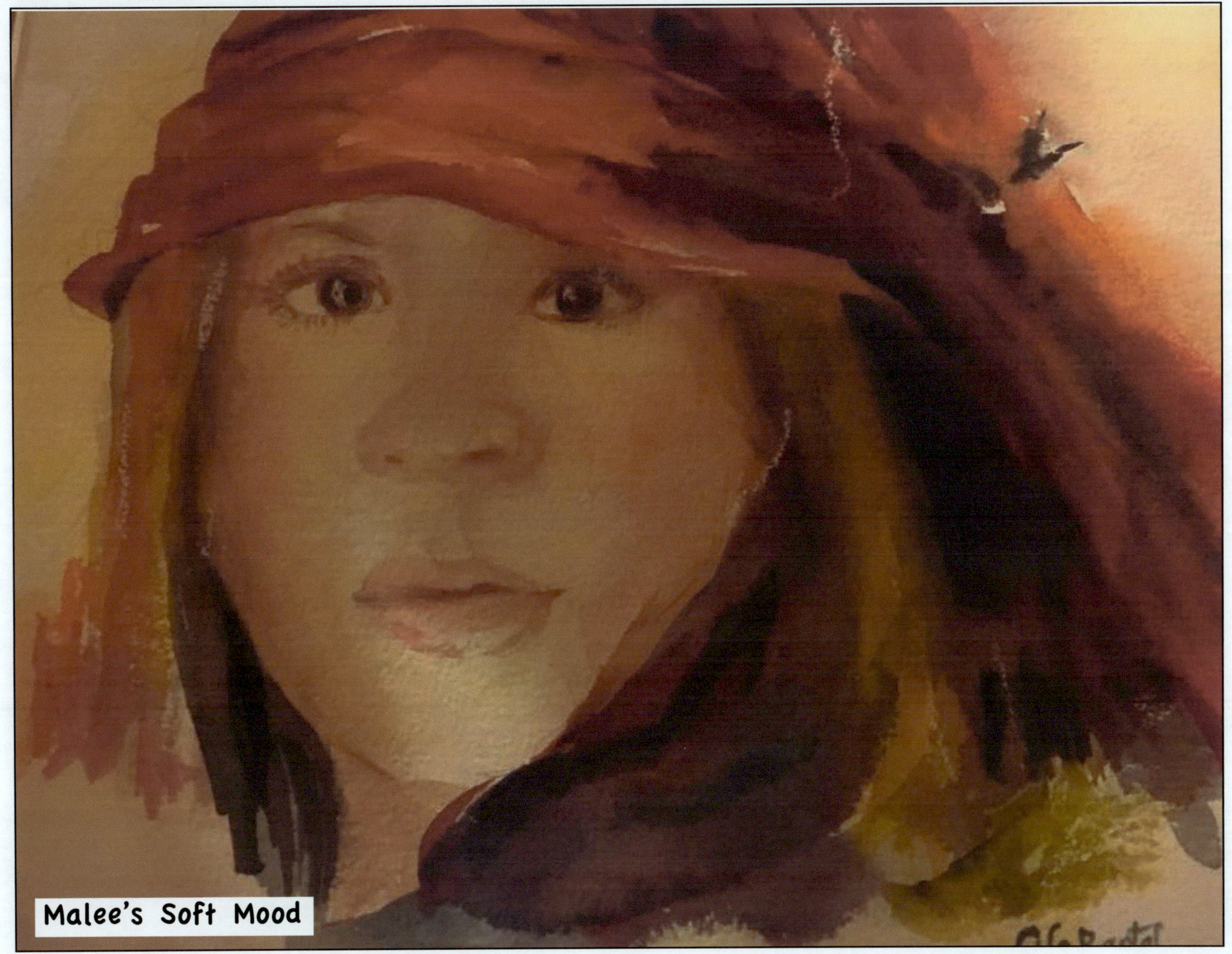

Malee's Soft Mood

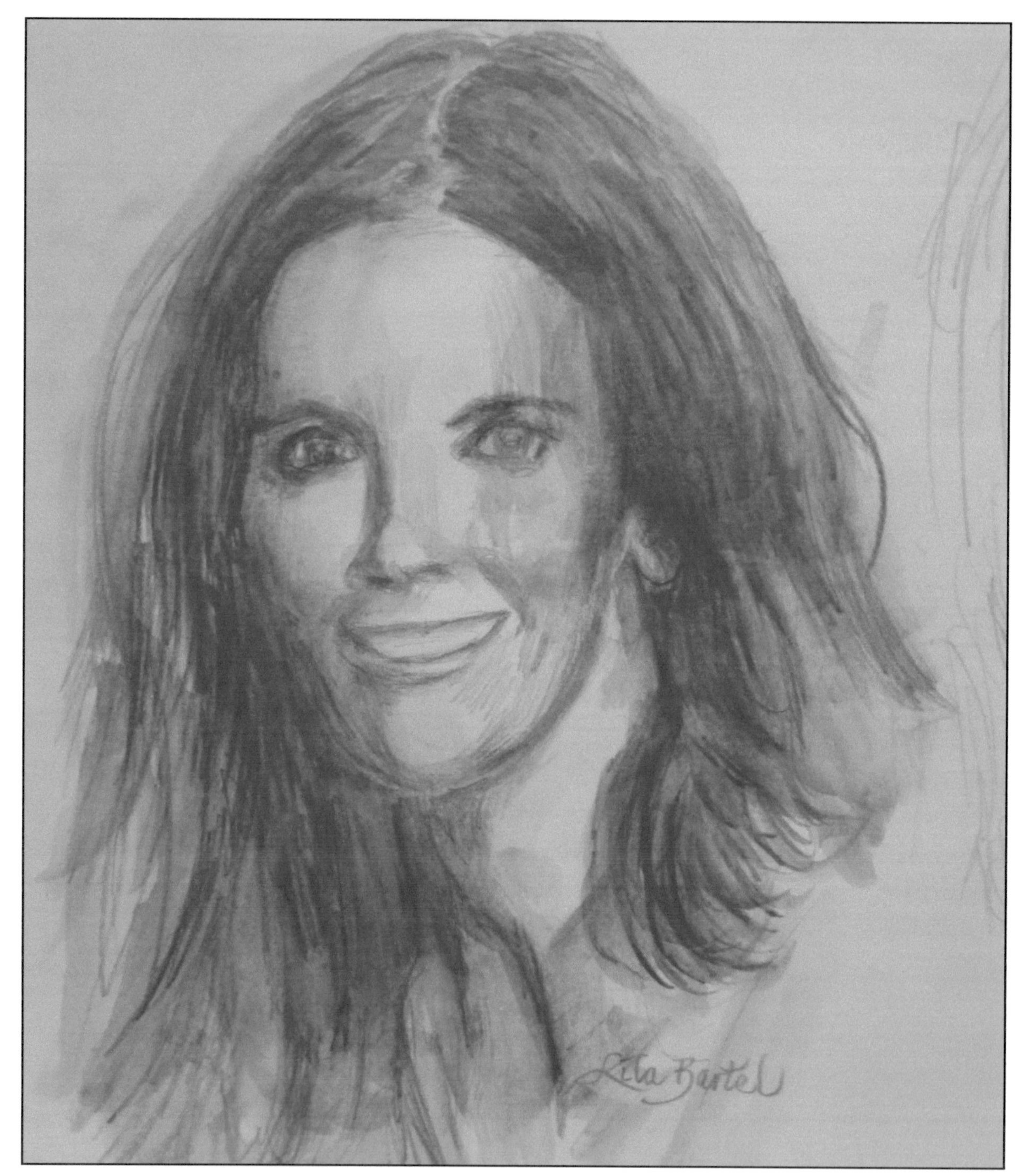

Subtle

Subtle Fragrance

She prefers her fragrances
subtle.

Her parents raised a farm girl,
intelligent, organized

family values thriving
on the prairie soil

and rooted in faith
that taught her

whatever the moment calls for
is what we're called to do.

So, she learned to uplift the elderly.

Grateful for the Journey

I've come to believe my restless heart

will one day find its home

on Paradise.

I imagine the voyage

long and thrilling,

I muse about the countless souls I'll meet,

I think of all the things I'll learn

on every world I visit,

and I'm grateful for the journey.

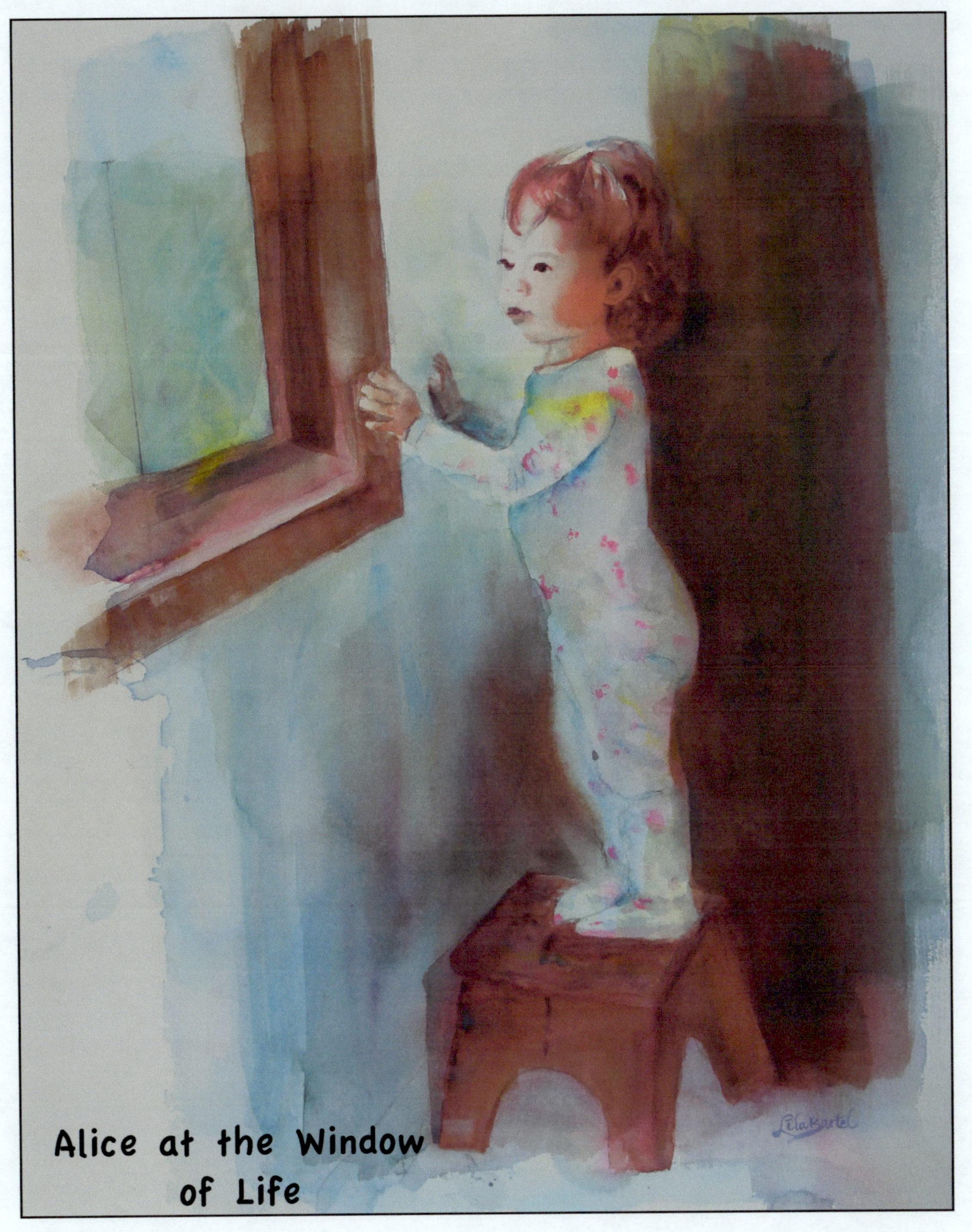

Alice at the Window
of Life